CW00832030

NATHAN MILLWARD was born and raised in the UK. He studied business and management at university, and went on to work in marketing, PR and journalism. After writing for university and local papers he found regular work as a car reviewer/road tester for an automotive magazine in England. Having worked freelance for a while he decided to head to Australia on a whim. This is his first book.

Visit Nathan Millward's website at

www.thepostman.org.uk

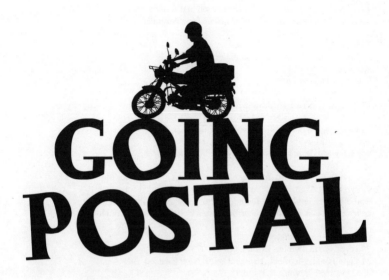

GOING POSTAL

NATHAN MILLWARD

ABC
Books

ABC Books The ABC 'Wave' device is a trademark of the Australian Broadcasting Corporation and is used under licence by HarperCollins*Publishers* Australia.

First published in Australia in 2011
by HarperCollins*Publishers* Australia Pty Limited
ABN 36 009 913 517
harpercollins.com.au

Copyright © Nathan Millward 2011

The right of Nathan Millward to be identified as the author of this work has been asserted by him under the *Copyright Amendment (Moral Rights) Act 2000.*

This work is copyright. Apart from any use as permitted under the *Copyright Act 1968*, no part may be reproduced, copied, scanned, stored in a retrieval system, recorded, or transmitted, in any form or by any means, without the prior written permission of the publisher.

HarperCollins*Publishers*
25 Ryde Road, Pymble, Sydney, NSW 2073, Australia
31 View Road, Glenfield, Auckland 0627, New Zealand
A 53, Sector 57, Noida, UP, India
77–85 Fulham Palace Road, London W6 8JB, United Kingdom
2 Bloor Street East, 20th floor, Toronto, Ontario M4W 1A8, Canada
10 East 53rd Street, New York NY 10022, USA

National Library of Australia Cataloguing-in-Publication data:

Millward, Nathan.
Going postal : the ups and downs of travelling the world on a postie bike / Nathan Millward.
1st edition
9780733328060 (pbk.)
Millward, Nathan – Travel.
Motorcyclists – Biography.
Motorcycle touring – Personal narratives.
Travelers – Biography.
910.4092

Cover and internal design by Natalie Winter
Back cover photos by Nathan Millward
Typeset in Bembo 11/17pt by Letter Space
Printed and bound in Australia by Griffin Press
70gsm Classic used by HarperCollins*Publishers* is a natural, recyclable product made from wood grown in sustainable forests. The manufacturing processes conform to the environmental regulations in the country of origin, Finland.

5 4 3 2 1 11 12 13 14

For Mum and Dad

Contents

Maps

Preface

This is the story of my motorbike trip across the world. It took place from January to September 2009, on a little Honda called Dorothy. She's a brilliant bike, painted red, the colour of speed, though she herself is not very fast. One time we hit eighty-five kilometres per hour and almost crashed with excitement.

I say 'we' because it's me and her. The two of us, who one day hit the road and never turned back, not until we'd ridden 35,000 kilometres in nine months, through eighteen countries in a single pair of basketball boots and with gloves that seldom matched.

But that doesn't matter. The road knows no fashion sense and neither did we. We were just riders, of no fixed abode, pushed by the most incredible urge just to get there, the other side of the world. Leaving on a whim, no planning, no preparation. Just go.

But this journey doesn't start with a motorbike, or even the open road. No, as you might well expect with a story of this nature, it begins with a woman, who for the sake of this book we shall call Mandy. If it wasn't for Mandy there would be no adventure, no Dorothy and certainly no story to tell. There would just be me, in an office cubicle somewhere, looking out of the window knowing there's something else out there but not having the faintest idea what.

I met Mandy in Sydney, at speed-dating of all places. She was the beautiful blonde with good style on table six. I was the scruffy Englishman on a working holiday visa with dirty glasses who came over with a bottle of beer; and the first thing she said was, 'Where's mine?' It wasn't the best way to start the three minutes we had together, but it couldn't have been that bad, because at the end of the night she ticked my box and I ticked hers. We went out a few days later, and just clicked, connecting in a way that at times felt as though we were held together by a bungee rope.

We'd pull apart as far as we could until the rope twanged and we shot back together with a bang. To me she was a challenge, strong-headed and stubborn … about me she said the same. Yet we both hung on in there, through the good times and the bad, the worst of which was when we were on opposite sides of the world for five months, because if there's one thing guaranteed to get in the way of a good relationship, it's a visa.

In fact it was during that five months apart, me in my native England, Mandy in her adopted home of Australia, that I came up with the idea for this trip. It's flying, you see. I hate it. And so when I finally accepted that life on the other side of the world really wasn't much fun without her, I figured rather than fly back to Australia, I would ride there by motorbike instead.

I had three reasons for thinking this to be a good idea. First, I like motorbikes. Second, I like travelling. Third, a friend of mine called Thomas Wielecki once told me how a big motorcycle trip like this can change you. He never said how or why or in what way, just that it happens. And I quite liked the sound of that.

Immediately I went out and bought the perfect machine for the trip. It was a Honda C90, painted baby blue, a step-through. It cost five hundred quid. I realise that's a far cry from what Ewan McGregor and Charley Boorman were going around the world on at the time, but it was the most reliable bike I could afford. And the colour matched my eyes. From there I began to research exactly what documents I'd need and the route I would take. From England, through Europe, to Iran and Pakistan and India, then across to Thailand and down through Malaysia and Indonesia until finally Australia, and Mandy's doorstep.

For a while it really seemed like I was going to give this thing a go. I told my parents and friends. They all thought it was ridiculous, but I was adamant, I was going to do it, right up until the point at which I asked my nan what she thought. Her advice was that if I wake up in the morning and still know it's the one thing I want to do, then go off and do it. But, she said, if you wake up with the slightest hint of doubt, then maybe it's not the right thing after all.

I woke up the next morning and it didn't feel right. I couldn't possibly wait however many months I assumed it would take to ride across the world before seeing Mandy again. I had to see her that minute, that second, so I gave up on the idea to ride across the world on a motorbike, quit my job in London, booked a ticket and flew back to Australia the following week.

'What are you doing here?' Mandy asked the day I surprised her on the ferry she took to work.

'I've come here for you,' I said, the Opera House now in view. I'd not told her I was coming, just in case she told me not to.

And so began an eight-month period together in Sydney, back in the place where it all began. Great times: holding hands, walking on the beach, the waves at our feet. Going back to Australia was the best thing I ever did. The only problem was that in my haste to get there I'd only been able to get a short-term visa, so ended up making sandwiches in a café.

It wasn't an easy time for either of us. Mandy wanted stability, knowledge of a future, some nice living room furniture; all I had to offer was leftover lasagne from the café and the troubles of an uncertain situation. But we tried, dear lord we tried; we tried to the point at which we surprised ourselves that we were still, well, trying. And then the whole thing came crashing down the day I went to ask Immigration for an extension on my visa. 'No, it's time for you to go,' was the reply. Be gone in no more than twenty days.

And that's where this story begins.

1

Going Home

Sydney

I sat in the centre of Sydney waiting for the lights to turn green. In the reflection of a shop window a familiar image was staring back at me. It was typically English — collared shirt, bad teeth, bad hair, terrible combat shorts. But then I looked down at Doris, the decommissioned 105cc Australia Post bike, and felt instantly cool again. She was red, like they all are, with four semi-automatic gears and an orange milk crate strapped to the back. I gave her a gentle rev, just a tickle. The light turned green. Go.

Flat out in first, the speedo firing like a rocket until the moment I clicked her into second and on the wave of acceleration continued, past Town Hall and down the hill beyond. Pedestrians ran for their lives, darting left and right in a bid to get out of the way of this flying red machine. Third gear now, past Darling Harbour to our right and the Powerhouse Museum to our left, traffic streaming in every direction, the pair of us blaring down the centre, my eyes alert, spider sense tingling: don't you dare step out, don't you dare pull out.

On to the freeway now, dodging the traffic on the inside lane over the brow of Anzac Bridge and down the other side, the blue water below. I loved this bit of the journey, flat out at seventy-five kilometres per hour and weaving between cars and lorries until hard right at the bottom then up the hill towards Rozelle. Nothing less than full throttle, Doris's 105cc chest beating as though it was about to explode and the pair of us squeezing between cars and buses as they waited at the traffic lights. At the top of the hill we turned down Darling Street and jinked through a series of narrow side streets, always riding the racing line and not braking for the house until it was almost too late.

'How did you get on?' Mandy asked as she greeted me at the door.

'Not good,' I said, 'I've got to be out of the country in twenty days.'

We hugged. I took off my helmet and gloves and followed her into the house. The corridor was cool and dark compared to the bright roaring light outside. My old Converse boots made the floorboards clatter as they led a familiar trail through to the kitchen at the back of the house, where the back door was open and the heat of a Sydney summer's day came blazing in.

We sat down around the kitchen table and drank a cup of tea. If I tried to write the words to accurately reflect the mood at this moment, the page would be blank, because for a while we sat in silence, nothing much to say but 'What are you thinking?' And the other one saying, 'I was just thinking how shit this all is.' And the other one nodding, and then sipping their tea. Though if we were being completely honest, there was probably a part of both of us that day that saw this as a blessing in disguise. It simply hadn't worked out. My plan to come back and make things work had failed.

Love certainly wasn't the problem. There was plenty of that. It was more the background to it, the uncertainty, and the visa. We just wanted to let the relationship breathe and develop at its own pace, without the pressures of an uncertain situation. Everything we tried seemed to fail, every door that momentarily opened again slammed shut. And the longer I had to work in the café, the longer the uncertain situation dragged on, the harder it became. We talked about marriage but were reluctant to have it seen as something done for a visa, though it wouldn't have been just for that.

Mandy was the person I never realised existed. The one that smashes your defences to smithereens and leaves you completely exposed. You are revealed for all that you are and all that you are not. Sometimes that was painful but sometimes that was nice. I guess she was my mirror and I was hers. Often the reflections were so ugly we would try to look away, but when the person you care so desperately about is the one holding the mirror that's not something so easily done. So you look and you see yourself, warts and all. And strangely that was addictive.

Whose idea was it to solve this sticky situation by getting me to ride home on a motorbike, on Doris? Well, it was Mandy's, much to my surprise. I was leaning against the stove, trying to figure out what to think and what to do, when Mandy suddenly blurted out, 'Well, why don't you ride home?' Of course I'd told her of my original plan to ride from London to Sydney on a motorbike and sweep her off her feet when I got here, including my reasons for wanting to do it, but not for a minute did I think she would present it as an option that day.

'No chance,' I answered. 'For a start I don't have the time, I don't have the money, and on what, Doris? She'd never make it.' No, it was a silly idea, one not even worth thinking about. In the space of twenty days, I'd have to prepare the bike, sort out all the visas and other documents, buy and pack the equipment, then ride almost 5000 kilometres across Australia to Darwin where I knew a boat would be able to take me to East Timor. All that in twenty days. It wasn't possible, for three reasons.

First, the lack of time. I calculated that at Doris's seventy-five-kilometre-per-hour maximum cruising speed we would need two and a half weeks to ride to Darwin, with a day at that end to sort out final details and get her on the boat. Twenty minus seventeen, minus one, equals two … that's how many days we would have to transform me and Doris into a pair of sturdy explorers ready for a ride across the world. A book I once read advised allowing at least a year to prepare for such a trip. Two days. That's all we would have.

Second, the lack of money. The café didn't pay me much, and scribbling down numbers on the back of an envelope confirmed I'd got $2000 left on one credit card, $3000 on another, $1000 under the mattress, and I was still owed a couple of grand from some work I'd done on the side. That made $8000 of accessible funds. I didn't know if that was going to be enough, and in truth had no real way of knowing. I could only guess at how long it would take and how much I'd need to spend along the way, based on the calculations I'd made first time around.

And third, the state of Doris, the postie bike I'd bought for $1400 a few months earlier from a man in Newcastle. I'd got the train up there and ridden her back down, along the Pacific Highway, flat out in the rain for hours on end. Not many weeks later she began to make a funny noise, hence her appointment with the mechanic in a few days. Her back wheel was also missing a spoke, her headlight didn't always work, she leaked oil, and one of the exhaust guard mounts had broken off and was held on by wire. She was all right for the city but I wouldn't want to ride her much further.

If those three reasons weren't enough, there was also the small matter of it being the wet season in the north, my parents' known opposition to the idea, my lack of mechanical skill and riding ability, not to mention that after Australia we were talking about riding a 105cc semi-automatic postie bike across Indonesia, Malaysia, Thailand, Nepal, India, Pakistan, Iran, Turkey and Europe, on a route that, while well-trodden by overland travellers, is still by no means an easy, safe or predictable one, especially without any planning.

Yet Mandy was right. One way or another I had to leave the country in twenty days, whether on the return air ticket I already had, or by motorbike. And the more I thought about it as we stood in her kitchen that day, the more I thought, 'Yeah, she's right. I do need to do this because if I don't I'll find myself in later life forever wondering why I didn't set off on that motorbike that day.' I mean, how many times does life present you with such an opportunity? No commitments, nothing to go back to, no job, no kids, no mortgage. The only thing I had in my life was her. And she was telling me to do it.

But it wasn't just that. In a way I didn't know where else to go or where else to be. If I flew home to England people would ask what I was doing back and why things hadn't worked out in Australia. I didn't really want to answer those questions or face the reality of it myself. It hadn't worked out because ... me, us, the situation ... I don't know. Now it was a sense of wanting to disappear, get lost, embark on a journey and undertake a terrific challenge, to clear my head, to sort things out, in the hope that things would somehow be easier, be better, I would be *better*, when, or if, I ever made it to the other side. And so the motorcycle idea suddenly had a new purpose to it, a point. And I didn't need much convincing about that.

I put my head in my hands and took a deep breath. Did I really have this in me, could I really do this, was I really capable of riding across the world on a postie bike with only two days' planning and no clue as to whether I had enough money to make it to the end? Probably not. But if I didn't give it a go I wasn't sure what else I would do. Fly home to England, having to explain why I was back? No. And so with that, I cut the rope, and fell.

For the next two days we scribbled a dozen lists and ran the length of Sydney ticking them off. I bought a cheap tool set from Bunnings, some spare oil, a set of instant tyre inflators and a huge aluminium box from Supercheap Auto to bolt on the back. Neighbours Pete and his son Louis helped drill and fix the box to Doris's rear rack. Mandy donated her pocket knife and sleeping bag; her housemate Sal bought me a waterproof map of Australia on which we worked out the best route — up the east coast, not the red centre — while her boyfriend Matty set me up with a pair of welding gloves to ride in. They were beige, with blue piping around the cuff. Another friend, Rowan, came over later with a spare pair; these were leather with silver metal studs.

After that I rode to the army store on York Street to look at hunting knives, camping equipment, tents, that sort of thing, none of which I had a budget for. Instead I bought a three-litre water pouch and a second-hand roll mat from a charity shop for a couple of dollars. For true bargains I hit the cheap Chinese store near Central Station, buying scissors, a money belt, bungee ropes, a plastic sign that said 'no junk mail' to stick on Doris's box, not to mention a sewing kit which I thought I might need. I stopped at the chiropractor's in Bondi to treat my back then to the café, where I'd already finished, to say goodbye. I don't think they believed me; no one believed me.

One day down, one to go. Day Two.

The next morning I rode to Glebe market to pick up some last-minute things. As I was putting my helmet on I saw Kevin Rudd get out of his car and go inside a bookshop across the road. This is an omen, I thought, so I followed him with my helmet and asked his security guard if the Prime Minister of Australia would mind signing it as I was riding to England the next day on a postie bike. Mr Rudd was mildly baffled by my disturbance as he browsed through a book, but obliged anyway: 'All the best, K. Rudd, P. Minister,' he wrote upside down. I walked away chuffed until I realised I should have asked him for a visa.

I double-checked what documents I might need before cancelling Doris's appointment with the mechanic because there was no time. The shipping company told me there was a cargo boat leaving Darwin for East Timor one day before my visa expired. To compensate, I reduced my riding time to sixteen days and made a mental note to ride like the wind because ships to East Timor only sail every ten days and if I missed that one I would be in trouble with Immigration. I bought a five-litre jerry can from the BP garage on Darling Street, tightened Doris's chain with my new tools, had a few goodbye drinks in the back garden with a group of friends, and that was it, planning done. Leave the next morning.

The alarm clock blew early, about 6 a.m. It was a strange moment waking up that day. The smell of adventure in the air, a pile of bags and bits to be packed in the corner of the room, and Mandy lying beside me, who I would soon be leaving behind. The pair of us had remained completely numb throughout all this, neither of us willing to acknowledge that I would be gone that day. 'It'll be all right,' we'd continued to tell ourselves, which I imagine is quite a normal thing to do in circumstances such as these, you know, about to ride a bike across the world. We ate a breakfast of Vegemite on toast, and tea. It would be the last time we sat around the same kitchen table for a while. We didn't have a plan for the future; we were just going to wait and see.

Dashing about the house, it was a case of pack this, fold that, room for this, no room for that. The aluminium box was mounted wrong. Back to Rowan's workshop to borrow tools to drill four new holes and tape up those now wrong. By the time we made it back to the house it was 11 a.m. and I was already three hours late getting on the road. In the back garden I bungee-roped the milk crate on top of the box to carry oil and spare petrol cans that were now brimful. Everything else went in the lockable aluminium box, or, like my tool kit, roll mat and thongs, strapped to the outside, exposed to the elements. I gave Doris one big rock to make sure it didn't all fall off.

A bright bolt of sobriety struck me as I manoeuvred Doris from the back garden to the launch pad out front. The weight was stacked far too high and even in a straight line I struggled to keep her upright. This didn't fill me with much confidence, but it was too late to worry about it; I had to hit the road, time was ticking away and that boat out of Darwin now left in just seventeen days. Doris *had* to be on it, and so leaning this way and that, I guided us around the corner and parked outside the house. By now everyone had gathered at the gate to witness the departure of the person they expected to be back in time for dinner that same night. No one expected me to get very far.

On my feet I wore a brand-new pair of blue basketball boots, on my hands the beige welding gloves donated by Matty, across my chest a white T-shirt reading 'Canada' (because that's Mandy's home country), on my legs a pair of skater trousers I'd bought to ride my skateboard that had recently been crushed beneath the wheels of a bus on Oxford Street, while on my head sat a bright white helmet, which despite being signed by Kevin Rudd still made me look like Marvin from *The Hitchhiker's Guide to the Galaxy*.

Then there was Doris, a clapped-out Honda CT110 with a spoke missing in the back wheel, an oil leak with no traceable source and a clatter from her engine that sounded like stones going round in a dryer. 'Clatter, clatter, clatter,' she went as the shocked neighbours looked on wondering where the English guy next door was off to. But for once even her headlight was working and her bald back tyre hadn't gone flat. The pair of us looked like real bags of shit. But we'd done our best in the two days we'd been given and now we were ready to see if determination alone really was enough compensation for everything else we lacked. I hoped it would be. It's all we had …

Nothing else to do now but say goodbye. We were by the kerbside, packed and loaded, looking on, down the street, the open road, wondering where it would lead and whether we'd actually make it beyond the city gates before turning around and heading back. Mandy joined me at the kerb, the hardest day. This was it, after all that'd been. Where would I be if it wasn't for her; not sitting here in Sydney, that's for sure. The sky above wouldn't be an Aussie blue but an English grey, I wouldn't know Doris and I wouldn't now have a story to tell. As Doris purred beneath my knees the tears rolled down our cheeks. See you in a thousand weeks.

2

Crazy Days

Leaving Sydney

This then was it, no turning back, ride as fast as I dare, the wind in my hair and the sun beating down. It really was the most baffling of all days. I couldn't tell you what I was thinking, a bit of everything I suppose. Happiness, sadness, fear, excitement, doubt, freedom. Doris beneath me, roaring her poor little head off as she struggled to tug all that weight along. But cope she did, for as the arch of the Harbour Bridge rose above our heads we were already up to seventy kilometres per hour and even passing some traffic along the way.

'Where's he off to?' I imagined the drivers of the cars thinking as I shot by with my head on the handlebars to keep the slipstream low. And then they would have read it, scribbled in felt-tip pen down the flanks of the aluminium box: 'From Sydney … to London.' Oh how they must have laughed, and I could have laughed with them, because it really was an absurd situation. Did I actually think I could make it across the world on Doris? Well, I was going to give it a damn good go.

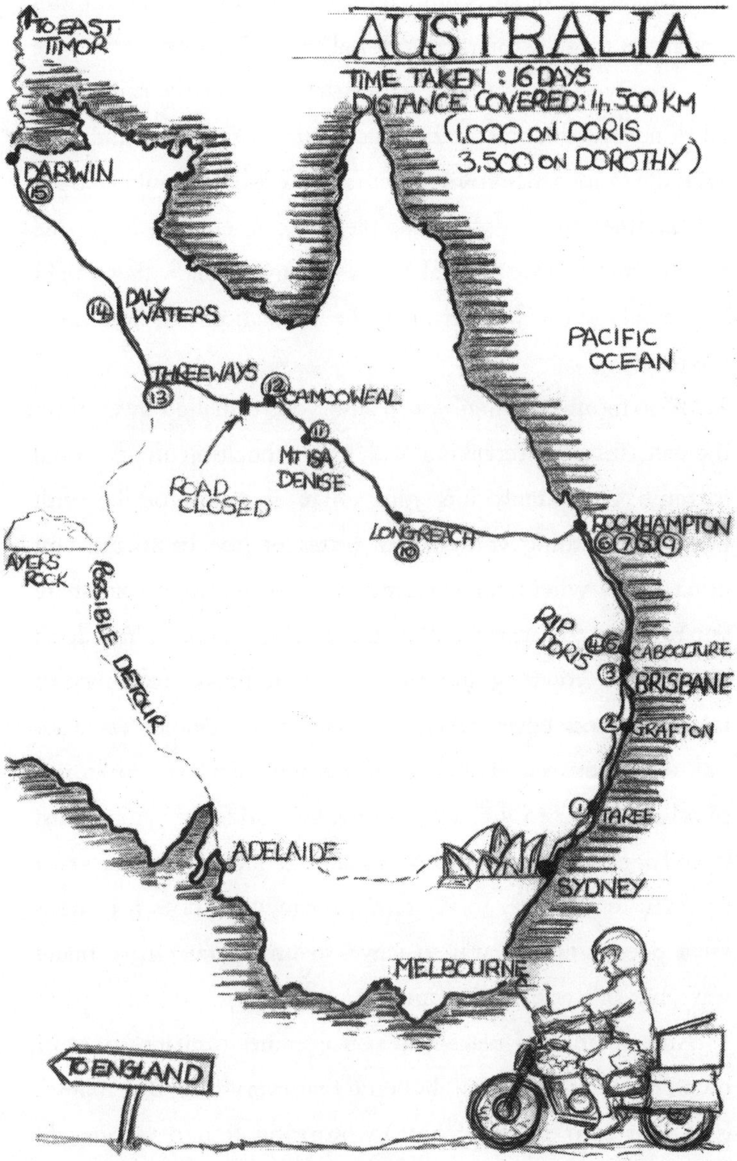

AUSTRALIA
TIME TAKEN : 16 DAYS
DISTANCE COVERED: 4,500 KM
(1,000 ON DORIS
3,500 ON DOROTHY)
TO EAST TIMOR
DARWIN
15
14
DALY WATERS
PACIFIC OCEAN
THREEWAYS
13
12
CAMOOWEAL
11
MT ISA
DENISE
ROAD CLOSED
ROCKHAMPTON
6 7 8 9
LONGREACH
10
AYERS ROCK
POSSIBLE DETOUR
RIP DORIS
4 5
CABOOLTURE
3
BRISBANE
2
GRAFTON
1
TAREE
ADELAIDE
SYDNEY
MELBOURNE
TO ENGLAND

In many ways, this first stage of the journey was going to be the hardest test of all. So much ground to cover, so little room for things to go wrong. I'd based all my calculations on a ride I'd recently made to Canberra for the Summernats car festival. I'd done that distance of 250 kilometres in six hours and rode back the same day. So twelve hours in the saddle would take me 500 kilometres. That would be plenty good enough to get me to Darwin in time and take care of any mishaps that might happen along the way. That was the calculation, but now came the reality.

That moment when you realise you've drifted away from the safe shore is terrifying and truly liberating in its brutal extreme. It suddenly hits you: you're on a motorbike with every single thing you own in boxes on the back, and you don't know where you're going to sleep that night or where you're going to eat or where you're going to get fuel. You don't know who you're going to call if you break down; every kilometre you cover takes you one stroke deeper into the unknown. You can read about it and you can hear the stories of what it's like to do such a thing, but suddenly being thrust into that position with barely any time to let it all sink in was a cold bucket of water to the face. I mean, what does it involve, what does it take? I was so naive, so unprepared in so many ways, but this was my life now.

And no more a place will you ever be in charge of your own destiny as out here. The sense that everything that follows is of your own doing, of your own organisation, decisions and shortcomings. Maybe that was the appeal, how everything depends on those two hands resting on the handlebars, the right one with the throttle to the stop. Your life, your future, your sanity. It's there and you feel the weight of it. That's what I mean by terrifying, because of course you doubt whether you're really capable. Of course you worry that you don't have it in you or that something is going to go terribly wrong.

What had worried me most in those two days of packing was that I might have second thoughts after I'd hit the road — what if I wanted to turn back, what if I realised just what a big mistake I was making? A bit like setting up your own business or walking down the aisle, I suspect. It was then some relief to find that as the road opened up and the towers of Sydney slid further and further behind I felt nothing but the urge to just keep riding, to see how far we could get, to give it everything I'd got. I knew turning around wouldn't solve a single thing so I put my head down and when a tear reached my lips I would lick it because it really was a hot day and I needed the fluid.

My route from here to Darwin was going to be a simple one. Up the coast to Rockhampton, turn left along the Capricorn Highway and through the Outback, join the Barkly Highway and then at Threeways junction turn right for our final run along the Stuart Highway into Darwin. Two turns in almost 4500 kilometres. I considered going up through the red centre, given that the distance was slightly shorter, but was keen to ride the coast, to see the sea and smell the salt air, to pass through Byron Bay and follow the path so many other travellers to this part of the world tend to tread, something I'd never found time to do in all the time I'd spent in Australia.

To be entering such a world on a motorbike was an incredible thing, feeling the sun on your face and the wind buffet you about. There is no interface, just man and machine, no glass, no sound but the engine you sit astride and the rumble of the tiny tyres on the road. I'd ridden and driven the road north of Sydney a few times before, but today it felt different; it felt like it had no ending and that if I put enough trust in it, it would take me all the way to the other side of the world, of course having to cross a couple of seas along the way. The only item I still didn't have was a tent.

I was reminded of that just as the sun began to set at the end of that first day when suddenly I wondered where I was going to sleep that night. I had a roll mat and a sleeping bag but nothing to put them under. That left me to consider the other options, and passing signs for Taree, 300 kilometres north of Sydney, I thought there must be a caravan site or motel there. And sure enough, Ray's Caravan Park had a vacancy sign twinkling in the dimming light and so I swung off the road and down the gravel drive. I brought Doris to a stand-still and entered reception, where I was immediately told about the road.

'It's closed,' said Ray as I paid for a caravan he was going to let me have cheap. He said far up north, deep inside the Northern Territory, the rain had been so bad that the road had been completely washed away. The road was now impassable, and the chances of it opening by the time I got there were pretty slim. I couldn't believe it at first — one road between Sydney and Darwin? As we studied the map of Australia on his wall, I asked about alternative routes, and he pointed towards Adelaide, suggesting I turn back and go that way, up through the red centre. It was a detour that would add at least 1000 kilometres to the distance and probably give us no chance of making that first boat.

It wasn't a tough decision because I knew if I turned around and went back via Sydney I would stop off there and probably never get going again, catching the plane home to England instead. I didn't want to do that. So I knew in my mind that whether the road opened or not I was just going to keep riding and let fate decide whether I would make that boat. If the road opened in time, then we would; if it didn't, then chances are we wouldn't, and no doubt that would leave me in big trouble with Immigration, but I thought it worth the risk. I ate takeaway chicken while studying the map with Ray on the bench outside the caravan. Then I went to sleep. My first night on the road.

It drizzled the next morning, though not enough to dampen the mood. I rode along singing and talking to myself, wobbling my head and jiggling to the music I had playing inside me. Heaven knows what the cars coming the other way must have thought. A big white bulbous ball stuck on the head of a madman in control of a motorbike that resembled a Wild West wagon loaded to the gills with all the gear needed to start a colony. I saw people stare, some beeped and stuck up their thumb, and I waved. To the man in the lorry who pushed me into the weeds I stuck up my finger and hoped he wasn't waiting for me at the next petrol stop as Doris was only managing a hundred kilometres to the tank and he might have flattened me.

Such moments, filling up with gas, always brought amusement. I would be there at the pump with Doris towering high with all her gear, and people would come over and say, 'You've ridden from Sydney on that!' I'd nod and tell them about my plan to ride to England, to which they'd respond, 'I can't believe you've ridden a postie all the way from Sydney … and you're going to Darwin! Here, Bruce, come and cop a load of this … this guy's riding his postie all the way from Sydney to Darwin.' Bruce would come over, shake my hand, ask where I was heading and I'd say England, and Bruce'd say, 'Darwin, I can't believe it.' And I would just smile and say, 'Yep, Darwin.'

Then I got my first puncture.

I was in Coffs Harbour, buying cream for my saddle-sore backside, when it happened. 'No problem,' I say to myself. 'I'm handy, I've got tools.' I spread them across the floor of a supermarket carpark like an old pro: spanners, screwdrivers, pliers and the big hammer to wallop things with. The one thing I didn't have were tyre levers. I'd thought about buying some back in Sydney, but to save money decided I could do the job with the screwdrivers instead. And that, it turns out, is a bit like trying to open a tin of beans with a spoon. I struggled for an hour, dripping sweat, bleeding at the knuckle, pissed off, sun scorching; I was pooped. That's when Dave showed up.

He was a wily old bloke, thin as a rake, wearing a dirty white T-shirt and a dark blue baseball cap pulled low over his weathered head. For decoration he had a big black pair of sunglasses and a thick ginger beard framing a nervous broad grin. He'd been driving by in his beaten-up Holden jalopy and, unlike all the other bastards who'd driven past staring but not caring to stop, had pulled over and asked if I needed a hand. 'Sure do,' I hollered. Ten minutes later he returned with his tyre levers. And there went the afternoon.

It turned out Dave had backpacked home from London to Sydney when his dreams of being a rock 'n' roll legend had bitten the dust back in the sixties. He thought I was stupid even thinking of going through Iran and Pakistan, even though he'd come through Afghanistan and loved it. I listened intently but didn't take too much notice, because those countries were still so far away that I couldn't even entertain the idea of actually getting to them.

It took two hours, three failed attempts and a trip to the bike shop for more patches before the repaired wheel was back on and we sat down on the grass with the cold beers I'd bought in celebration. We talked all sorts of rubbish, like two old blokes passing time in a bar. After the storm of the last few days it was nice to sit for a minute, hearing Dave explain things like how I should wrap my legs in cardboard in case I was attacked by snakes in the bush. I really liked the bloke. He'd had dreams and ambitions, and I admired how he'd made the transition to regular family life without any hint of bitterness, no regrets.

I covered just 300 kilometres on that second day, arriving in the town of Grafton. It was another night in a caravan, this one costing forty bucks, which I know doesn't sound a lot but the budget I was trying to stick to was half that a day, to cover food, fuel and accommodation. Clearly in Australia twenty bucks a day just wasn't going to be possible, but in Asia I was confident, well, hopeful, that it would be enough. But money was the least of my worries right now; I'd still not told my mum.

As far as my parents were concerned, I was still in Sydney trying to sort out my visa. I knew if I'd told them in advance they would have said, 'Grow up, settle down, get a job.' It was the law of their generation, and they would have made me feel so guilty that I might very well have agreed. Not because I do what my parents tell me, but because I find it very easy to let other people's fears talk me out of doing things I want to do. And I often think that's all advice is: other people telling you why *they* wouldn't do it, rather than understanding why *you* should.

That night I sent an email from my laptop using the free wifi in the local McDonald's. I explained how my idea to ride across the world on a motorbike was finally happening, and that it was too late to stop me because I'd already set off. I explained what it meant to me, and how taking a plane wasn't an option. I finished with the line, 'I love you', something we don't often say in our family because we're too shy to say it. And so the situation was rather liberating. All the protocol and tradition of our family had gone out the window. I could say what I thought because, why not, I'm on a motorbike and might get wiped out by a lorry in the morning. So say it now, say it while it matters.

After that I sent one to the people on my group email list. This marked the point of no return, as announcing to the world that you're going to try and ride a 105cc postie bike across the world leaves a huge amount of room for embarrassment should you ever fail, or quit. I imagine in such circumstances there will always be those people who will say, 'I told you so.' Perhaps I shouldn't have sent this email, not telling anyone until we were almost in England. But I figured I could use the fear of losing face to fan the flames if the fires ever burned dim. I know we shouldn't worry about what other people think, but I did, I do.

The next morning the phone rang; it was Mum, hysterical. 'What the bloody hell are you doing?' she screamed before I'd had a chance to say hello. I was outside a bike shop at the time buying tyre levers. I had to take my ear away from the phone. She wasn't exploding in an angry, violent way, just in a, 'I'm your mother and I spent too long in labour to let this happen,' kinda way.

Dad thought it was brilliant — at least that's what I gathered when I spoke to him briefly. But what else could he say? He was the one who got me into motorbikes in the first place, taking me and my brother Jason down to an old quarry for us to tear around on a little 50cc moped. I was probably five at the time and not very good. I always remember approaching a corner and not bothering to turn or to stop; I just kept on going, shooting straight on with Dad chasing after me shouting, 'Brake Nathan brake!' When he finally caught up with me he said how close I'd been to hitting the barbed-wire fence. He was right, but I wasn't aiming for the fence, I was aiming for the lane beyond to see where it might lead. I guess now, all these years later, I was about to find out.

With Mum back on the phone, I managed to reduce her fury to a simmer, explaining there would be no turning back and how she shouldn't worry, I would be all right. 'Fine,' she said. 'Well. You just be careful and if you need anything just ring.' With that we said goodbye. How incredible. My mum gets an email with news of her son riding across the world on a 105cc wotsit, she rings in hysterics and within five minutes is offering to do anything she can to help.

Not that they could do much to help us with our third problem in as many days. Doris still seemed to be performing okay, but now there was a really loud hollow knocking sound coming from her engine. I'd always known it wasn't wise setting off without getting her to a mechanic first, but I knew if I had and something serious had been diagnosed then I would have been given the perfect excuse for not setting off. And I didn't want that excuse as I knew how easily I would have taken it. That's why I'd shut my ears to Doris's grumblings, said, 'Sod it,' and off we'd set.

Now, though, she really did need assistance because she wouldn't make it far in this state. Fortunately, I knew just the place. In a little town called Caboolture, just north of Brisbane, there's a shop that sells and repairs only postie bikes. I'd found them on the internet and was going to call in there anyway for some spares and advice. It's one of the reasons I'd chosen this route over coming up the red centre. I was now more grateful than ever for that decision. My plan was to have

Doris fixed and be back on the road by midday at the latest. Three days later …

Joe, the owner of the shop, was a tall man, early fifties I'd say, wearing a collared short-sleeve navy shirt, matching shorts and a pair of black boots and socks. He ran the place with his wife, Katrina, and knew all there was to know about postie bikes. Joe came outside to take a look at Doris. I fired her up and there she sat, hollow-knocking louder than ever. 'Doesn't sound good,' he said. 'It's probably your bottom-end on its way out.' Damn.

I asked Joe if she might make it to Darwin. He scratched his chin and said she might. He told me a story about a guy who tried riding up to Cape York on a postie bike with the same problem. I asked what happened and he said it blew up before it got there. That kinda answered my next question, but I asked it anyway. 'What about England, Joe, will she make it to England?'

Joe stopped scratching his chin and looked at me funny. 'Mate, you've got absolutely no chance.'

I knew he was going to say that.

Joe was a patient man and if he thought I was a plank he didn't show it. Instead he presented me with three options. The first was to rebuild the existing engine, probably taking five days and costing $400.

'I don't have that much time,' I told him.

'All right, what about if I fit a reconditioned engine?'

That was going to take a couple of days and cost $700. That sounded better. I was going to do that. Then the bastard laid a turd on my toe by making a third and final suggestion that burrowed deep beneath my skin. And that was to trade in Doris for one of the more reliable bikes he had in his showroom. I laughed and said, 'I don't think so', but while he went off to serve another customer I had a look anyway.

There were rows of machines just like Doris, all decommissioned postie bikes waiting for new owners to ride them around the city and sometimes farms. They're tough, tiny little things modified for Australia Post to carry the extra weight of letters and parcels. With four gears and no clutch they're easy to ride. It was on one of these that my friend Thomas Wielecki had ridden all the way around Australia on a shoestring, and in telling me the story had, through many twists and turns, led to this, me being here, on the same type of bike, about to try and ride it across the world. I often wonder what the outcome would have been had I done it the other way, arriving in Sydney, on the C90, strong from my adventure across the world, the whole thing out of my system and perhaps more successful in finding a way to stay. Though who knows, maybe Mandy would have met someone else while I was on my way. Really, that's why I flew instead.

I stopped at one bike and admired it. She was small and red like all the others, but rather than just the standard five-litre fuel tank under the seat, this one had an extra eight-litre tank from a motocross bike mounted in the step-through. It also had a set of orange panniers, a tent rack on the front, two water bottles strapped to a polished engine guard and a sheepskin cover that was just like sitting on a cushion. She looked so much tougher and meaner than all the others. Not only that, she was in perfect condition, almost new, and that was with 40,000 kilometres on the clock.

'Why don't you take her for a spin?' Joe asked.

This was dangerous. I'd dropped by to get my bike fixed, not to buy another one. But I figured what harm could it do? From the very first moment I sat on that bike I knew I had to have it. The engine was so smooth and with all the additional equipment it felt like a much sturdier machine. It was almost as though someone knew I was coming, on Doris, and had purpose-built the perfect bike for riding across the world. Deep down, as much as I wanted to deny it, I knew I was kidding myself in believing Doris could make it all the way to England, but of this bike's ability, I had no doubt.

Back at the shop I did false sums to pretend I had enough money. Joe said he'd give me $700 trade-in on Doris, leaving me another $1700 to find. By this time it was late afternoon, so I said I'd sleep on it and get back to him in the morning. I borrowed his tent but couldn't put it up properly, so I went to the Kmart in town and finally bought my own for forty bucks. There was a campsite nearby, not far from the main highway and on the banks of a river. I put the tent up in the scorching heat and sat with my laptop in the shaded area, recording a video diary about the events that had unfolded so far.

I faced a real dilemma. I still didn't know if the road was going to open in time. It was fifty-fifty judging by the weather forecast and I knew that if it wasn't open in time, then buying a new bike would be a huge waste of money because I'd have to abandon it to get back to Sydney and catch the flight home the day my visa expired. However, if the road did open and we made it to Darwin in time, how long realistically could Doris continue without needing serious repair or replacement? And so in many ways it would be pointless to ride her any further whether the road opened or not.

The next morning I raced to the bike shop and gave Joe my credit card.

'Are you sure, mate?'

'Yep, let's do it.'

I spent the afternoon in the Transport Offices trying to register the new bike. Not being an Australian resident I had to put my address down as the bike shop. For a while it looked like it might not be possible. I had to cancel the existing registration, get a refund on that, then register the new bike in my name with a new number plate so that I had enough time to get to England before it expired. Then finally, with everything done, the new bike in my name, I fired the machine into life. It was now the end of Day Six. I'd covered just 977 kilometres. We had our work cut out if we were going to stand a chance of making that boat.

'Thanks Joe, you guys have been great,' I said as I saddled up.

'No worries, mate. Now you ride safe and let us know how you get on.'

'I will,' I shouted as I hooked first gear and drizzled out of the carpark.

'By the way,' Joe hollered after me. 'Her name's Dorothy.'

3

A Road to Nowhere?

Caboolture

I felt guilty leaving Doris behind. She may not have made it all the way to England or even as far as Darwin, yet this was a bike that at a moment's notice had transformed herself from city hack into world explorer. She's the bike I'd picked out of the crowd on eBay. She's the one I'd put a nervous bid in for and fretted over as the auction expired. She was the bike I'd caught the train to Newcastle to collect. She was the bike I'd thrashed around Sydney, gone to work on, showed off on, fell off from. She was my bike, and I was leaving her behind. To rot on a farm because that's all Joe said she was good for.

Now I'd bought Dorothy, or Dot for short, and taken a gamble. It was silly really; if that road didn't open I'd be stuck with a credit card bill for a bike I'd have to try and flog before I was kicked out of the country in two weeks' time. The sensible thing would have been to carry on with Doris and ditch her if the worst happened. I wouldn't have lost a bean then. But I had to be realistic: I needed a bike that was going to give me the best chance of making it to England. And that was Dot.

Because I was no mechanic. I could change oil and now felt confident fixing a puncture, but I didn't have the first idea how to check the valves or the timing or the carburettor. I'd always been interested in motorbikes but had never bothered to learn how to fix them or take them apart. I just rode them. All I hoped for the journey ahead was that I'd meet plenty of people more capable. And if I didn't, then I guess I would just have to learn, and learn very quickly too, because I was starting to have visions of being in the middle of Pakistan, the bike packing up and me having to ask around for a mechanic as the Taliban took shots at me.

People may wonder why I didn't buy a better bike when I had the chance. Why did I get another postie and not a BMW or something bigger? The simple truth is that I couldn't afford one. But also, define *better*. Postie bikes are notoriously tough, they're reliable and, while they lack performance, this trip was always going to be about endurance, not speed. And to be honest a postie bike suited me and was perhaps a reflection of my character — a bit slow and ponderous — and the fact that Dot was out of her depth would serve as a nice reminder that I was too, trying to ride a postie bike where no other had gone before. Though that's not entirely true.

By this point I'd been in touch with a couple from Perth who were attempting to do the same thing, only with two of them on the same bike ... with all their luggage! I found that incredible. Riding away from Joe's shop, Dot was already loaded to the gills and unable to carry much more, and there was their little bike, exactly the same but carrying an extra person. The last I'd heard, Nathan (we were almost identical — name, age, bike) and Aki were already in Thailand, taking it slow, with us hoping to catch up with each other along the way. Then no doubt we'd race towards the English finish line to see who could cross it first. Knowing they were attempting something similar made me feel more normal.

For now, though, I had to get back to my trip, and the next thing I needed was a document called a Carnet de Passage. This is the paperwork needed to take a vehicle abroad and works just like a passport. Stamp in, stamp out. The idea being to stop you selling your vehicle for profit while in a foreign country. Back in Sydney I'd called the RAC, the people who administer it, only to be told the document usually takes four weeks to process. However, if I was to apply for it in person at their branch in Rockhampton, 590 kilometres north of Caboolture, they might *just* be able to do it in a week. Rather than me wait for it to be processed, they said they could post it ahead for me to collect in Darwin, before putting Dot on the boat to East Timor that sailed now in just fourteen days. It was going to be tight.

With no time to waste, it was to Rockhampton I was heading now, my skin burning in the blazing sun as I followed the liquorice strip of a coastal road as it dipped down to the water's edge before twisting back inland through tree-lined canyons. I was having fun, waving at the European backpackers touring the east coast in rented camper vans and pulling in at the free Driver Reviver tea stops, where you'd get chatting with families heading up to the Gold Coast in their Falcons and Commodores. That's the great thing about travelling in Australia. Every hundred kilometres or so there's a stall giving away tea and biscuits for a donation to the Rotary Club or whichever charity is running it. Some people would give me sandwiches or bits for my bike, like tie-wraps; it was just a good experience.

Too good in fact. Because I rolled into Rockhampton thinking it was Day Eight when it was actually Day Nine. And that meant it was Friday, not Thursday, and so the offices of the RAC would be closed the next morning and not open again until Monday. This was a terrible mistake to make, one that would cost me three days. There wasn't much I could do about it, only wait; actually I was quite glad for the opportunity to stop and let it all sink in and compose myself for the journey ahead. So far it had been a whirlwind, with not a moment to make sense of it all. Sydney to London on a postie bike; how daft. Mandy was surprised I'd made it this far. Knowing how useless I am with tools, she thought I might have turned back the day I got the puncture. We spoke several times a day. Conversation got harder the further I rode away.

I began my weekend by unpacking everything and laying it out on the ground. I asked myself if I really needed three jumpers and nine pairs of underpants, or eight T-shirts and all those little fiddly bits in my Bunnings tool kit that didn't fit anything. I threw half of it away, and then tried to bring some order to my packing; clothes — clean and dirty — inside my right pannier, oil and all the spare parts Joe had set me up with in the left. In the lockable aluminium box that had been transferred from Doris, I kept all my electrical gear — camera, helmet camera, laptop, iPod, the metres of cable to go with it, the travel adaptors and my tools. I didn't have a first-aid kit, waterproof trousers, a towel, soap, a stove or a torch; I was going to manage without.

Two German backpackers, Alex and Tanya, put up their tent near mine. We got chatting, them telling me about the old Holden station wagon they'd bought to drive down from Cairns to Sydney. Just outside of Rockhampton it had broken down. The local mechanic reckoned it was the fuel pump, so he was having a go at fixing it. That left all three of us stuck here for the weekend, on a campsite by the river with crocodile warning signs but no sign of the real thing. I'm not convinced Australia actually has any dangerous animals at all. I wonder instead if it's a tale to scare off tourists, like the ghosts in *Scooby Doo*. If a crocodile did crawl out of the water, I imagine it'd just be the campsite's caretaker in a monster suit who'd later blame it all on those pesky kids.

One of the jobs I had to do over the weekend was to arrange travel insurance. My existing policy didn't cover 'motorcycle touring' and I was nervous of riding uninsured. A decade earlier, in France, I'd skied into a tree and broken my femur and pelvis, needing a helicopter to airlift me off the mountain. The bill for that was astronomical so it was fortunate I had good insurance. Thankfully I found a company that did cover 'touring' and also didn't mind that I was already outside my home country. At $500 it wasn't cheap, but it was only half as expensive as the bill I got for the Carnet on Monday morning. Yep, $1000 for the document to take a postie bike abroad. It troubled me to think that if the road didn't open in time I'd just wasted a grand and a half, plus the $1700 for Dorothy.

The lady behind the counter at the RAC office asked what address she should post the Carnet to in Darwin. That stumped me because I didn't know anyone there. I'd never been. Then I remembered the telephone number I had scribbled on the back of my map of Australia. I went outside and dialled it.

'Hi mate, you don't know me but I met your mum at a tea stop in Brisbane the other day. She said if I ever needed anything in Darwin to give you a call.' Silence, so I continued, 'Well I wondered if you don't mind me having some mail sent to you. I'll collect it in a week or so if that's all right?' The poor guy must have wondered who the hell was calling, but eventually he stirred.

'Sure thing mate, my mum said you might call, here's the address … '

I'd met his mother and stepfather the day before at one of those rest stops. At first they'd annoyed me with endless talk of the dangers that lay ahead: the rain, the spiders, the crocodiles, the heat, the Aboriginals, the floods, the flies, the trucks and the pies. I didn't need to hear it, even though it was perhaps time I should. Slowly they mellowed, and the conversation turned to other things, like family and jobs. That's when the lady had given me the number and said to call her son if I needed anything in Darwin. Now, I couldn't thank them enough. With my Carnet in place I had everything I needed. All I could do now was to head inland, along the Capricorn Highway, in the hope that in 1000 kilometres, at a point in the Outback just beyond the town of Camooweal, I would discover a road that had been repaired in time.

Cutting through the silent, sunless morning, we blasted out of Rockhampton at 4 a.m. It was dark, empty and desolate. The temperature was perfect and with only us on the road the sense of solitude hit hard for the first time. I suppose others would call it loneliness, but wherever we fell on that continuum I adored it. Just to be alone with your thoughts as the dark strip of highway stretched out ahead, the only noise being Dot's little engine thrumming softly away, and my iPod providing the soundtrack. Music to capture a mood; I had David Gray's *New Day at Midnight* playing, track twelve. But who would you listen to out here? A dark Australian morning, you on a motorbike alone in the desert, a challenge to get somewhere, a time limit to do so and the sun slowly rolling out of bed behind you.

You knew it was coming when the mirrors began to glow. Not bright and fiery, more a warm fuzz that would ever so slowly grow brighter and brighter. There wasn't any warmth yet. Just dim light building and stretching along the horizon until it exploded over the top, lighting up my helmet like a bulb. For the rest of the morning I'd watch it rise from behind — we were travelling west, remember — until it was above my head, making my face red and my body sweat. And then fourteen hours later it would set. Gone for another day. What an incredible realisation of scale. That me and Dorothy were so insignificant in all of this. Just a tiny ball of moving metal parts and pieces of pale sunburnt flesh. If we crashed tomorrow, that huge ball of fire would still rise and fall just as it always had. And still the music would play.

At a town called Emerald, 270 kilometres in from the coast, a group of Aboriginal kids came up to me and started asking questions. I spoke a few words and then rode off. I was afraid. But why? All they wanted to do was talk; they were friendly, full of curiosity. Why was I so rude? I wouldn't have been if they'd been white. I would have stopped and chatted until we said a friendly goodbye. Was I racist? Not to Africans or Asians, so why Aboriginals? Was it because of the things I'd heard, like the trucker who told me 'all they do is fuck and breed'? Or was it those I'd seen in Sydney, drunk, shouting, that had made me nervous?

For the rest of the way to Mount Isa, 1000 kilometres, I tried to figure it all out. I knew it wasn't rational, but like the poisonous spiders and snakes, people had warned me about Aboriginals. 'Don't go near them, they might bite.' But these hadn't, and neither did the others I met later near Tennant Creek. So why had I listened? Why hadn't I judged the kids for who they were? Instead I'd been taken over by the same irrational feelings as the trucker. I didn't understand these people; they looked different, acted different, and instead of being curious I'd been afraid. And now I was a little ashamed.

Rain fell. Deep dark clouds would wait for us on the horizon, taunting us as we approached. My tactic was to dress down, not up. Put on my shorts and swap the boots for a pair of thongs. That way the clouds could make me as wet as they wanted, as they often did, because ten minutes of sunshine later I'd be dry again. But what a time to see the Outback! With the rain, came life. The contrast between red dirt, green leaves and blue sky was wonderfully vivid. A picture with only three colours, painted by nature and ruined by the red Dot screaming through it. I trailed my feet through the puddles to remind myself what it was like to be a kid.

At one point, so much rain had fallen that the highway between Winton and Cloncurry was flooded, although still passable. I stood with a couple of young teachers, Brody and Sarah, on their way home to Mount Isa. They offered to put Dot in the back of their ute and carry her across. I thought about it but knew I couldn't do that. We were riding to England and that meant we had to keep Dot's wheels on the ground as much as we could. No one would have known we were cheating except me and the teachers, but that was the point. I had to do it the proper way, to make it count. Instead, then, we waded through these flooded stretches of road, a hundred metres long, gauging how deep they were and then, with my feet dragging through the water, slowly crawling through in first gear, looking out for the caretaker in his crocodile suit.

On the other side, the teachers asked if I wanted to crash on their sofa that night. I looked at the violent sky and thought it was a good idea. I arrived on their doorstep two hours later, dripping wet. Their housemate Jason cooked spaghetti bolognaise that evening. After a week and a half of living on burgers and deep-fried finger food, it was nice to eat with a knife and fork, have a shower, drink a beer, watch some TV. And then I drifted off to sleep on their sofa.

The next morning I rode into Mount Isa town centre in search of the tourist information office to get an update on the road, the closure now only a couple of hundred kilometres ahead. The town was a complete contrast to anywhere else I'd seen in Australia. This wasn't a port city or a tourist town, but a mining community, much like the one in which I'd grown up in England with its huge black mounds of coal tailings looming over it like a dark spectre. I wouldn't say Mount Isa was a nice place, nor would I say it was horrible, it was just a town that reflected the industry that fuelled it. Same with the people. They were miners, like my dad. Tough skin, rough hands, dirty boots.

When I finally found the right building I walked inside and approached the lady on the information desk. This was the moment of truth. Make or break. 'Is the road to Darwin open?' I asked.

'Yes my dear, it opens to light traffic in the morning.'

I sat down in the café and ordered a pot of tea. Mixed emotions, I suppose. In a way I now wished the road had stayed closed, then I would have had my excuse to go back and spend the last few days in Sydney with Mandy because I missed her. Instead it opened, and on I had to go.

The waitress, Denise, brought over the tea. She was pleasant and cheerful, like the women who worked in the bakery where we bought our lunch as school kids. The sandwiches at the other shop were always bigger and cheaper, but it was the way these ladies made you feel — welcome, not a hindrance. It's why we went there. Denise was like those ladies.

We got chatting, about the road and where I was going. I explained the nature of the trip and how I came to be sitting at one of her tables with a dazed look on my face. After a while she disappeared and came back with a $50 note. 'By the sounds of it, you're going to need this more than I am.' I didn't know what else to say but 'Thank you.'

Before I left, Denise also offered me some advice: 'If you ever find yourself in danger and in need of some assistance,' she started, 'just ask for the fairies and they shall come.' In any other circumstances I might have considered her completely crackers and would have struggled not to tell her that, but right here, Day Thirteen, almost 3000 kilometres covered, 1600 to go in Australia — then the rest of the world — I wanted to believe in them as well. In fact already I believed in fairies. Dave was one. Joe was another. Who knows how many more I might meet between here and England?

The road opened next morning, and off I went, those remaining kilometres to be covered in just three days. The hours passed and the sun soared. We passed the point at which the road had been closed, the hole in it — now patched up — was massive, like a bomb crater. We rode on. Hour after hour. Face burning red, one of Joe's old T-shirts tied across it, my nose in the armpit, flies in my eyes, hardly any traffic here. You wave when you see someone else on the road. Signposts point to communities down dusty tracks. Who the hell lives out here? How did the early settlers ever cross this place? Nothing, and I mean nothing, around. Only the birds in the sky, the bush and the desert and the sense it will never ever, not for a minute, come to an end.

After a night feeding mosquitoes at the Threeways Homestead, we turned right, noses pointed towards Darwin. Full tanks, empty stomach, red face, watery eyes, *determined* watery eyes. A couple in a car I'd been leapfrogging ever since Mount Isa pulled over some distance ahead of me and flagged me down. They shared a coffee from their flask and cut me a piece of fruit cake. Fellowship of the road. I was standing, they were sitting in the car, Dot was parked up beside their car, nothing but sand and dirt for miles around. Another car blasted past. I scratched my growing beard, acknowledged my new life on the run. I passed back the plate and cup. They told me the road up ahead might also be closed because of the rain. I heard them but didn't care. By now I was a lightning bolt of determination, prepared to swim with Dot on my back or flap my wings hard enough to fly us both over any obstacle. We had to get there.

At the small community of Daly Waters, the rain drove me from my tent and into a caravan for the night. I ate a steak sandwich in the bar before returning to my room where I caught five minutes of a religious channel on the television. Someone was reciting a poem about a man who'd been struggling with life and who looked back to see just one set of footprints in the sand. This made him question why God hadn't been there with him to help. To which the presenter said, 'There was only one set of footprints because God had been carrying him on his back all along.'

I turned off the telly and thought what nonsense, robbing the man of his achievement like that. I wondered how I'd feel if I made it to England and someone tried to do that to me. Then I walked outside and saw the tyre marks in the dirt. With that in mind, I have to confess to being quite glad that Doris had to be retired. She may have had more soul and lived life a little closer to the edge. She was faster, louder, ruder, more like Dot's teenage son than her sibling. Dot was more of a plodder, slow and steady, like a turtle, but she was sure-footed and reliable. I missed Doris's charm, but no way would I have given Dot back. Not now, not on the final push along the Stuart Highway.

That day was a big one, those 589 kilometres all in one go: more sun, more rain, more flies, more pies. At a service station I met an English guy called Roy in an old MG sports car who was driving around the world. He gave me advice on Iran and Pakistan, and said he wouldn't try and talk anyone out of it, but he told me to be careful. I rode on, gritted teeth, the fire in my belly raging and with a dogged determination that we were going to do this, come hell or high water. We stopped in Katherine to buy some bread and bananas to make a sandwich, and I filled the tanks for the final push as that fireball roared and soared overhead and the traffic began to thicken and the signs for the city with a boat waiting at its clock began to count us down from 200 kilometres to one. And then, there it was.

Darwin.

Sunday 25 January, at around the same time normal folk would be having their evening dinner, me and Dot sauntered through the city gates, two weary travelling slags on the point of collapse, Dot with a bald tyre and in desperate need of fluid, me in a frazzled-eyed state with buttocks I could barely sit on. There was no champagne or party girls, just quiet, sombre relief. Eighteen days after my appointment with Immigration, two days before my visa ran out, we'd made it. Alive. On a different bike, having navigated flooded plains and sticky situations by the slimmest of margins. That night I slept at a campsite on the outskirts of town and it rained so hard the tent flooded. I woke beneath the barbecue stand.

That morning I went over to the stranger's house to collect the Carnet I hoped would have arrived by now. Carl was his name, a nice bloke, with a guard dog that bit my ankle and made me bleed. He said my documents hadn't turned up yet. I panicked because without a Carnet I wouldn't be able to put Dot on the boat, and if I couldn't put Dot on the boat, then I couldn't leave the country before my visa expired the day after next. I asked Carl to call me if anything arrived and rode back into town to find a doctor to give me the necessary injections for travelling through Asia — rabies, malaria, hepatitis and typhoid — plus a tetanus jab for the dog bite.

The next day my phone rang. It was Carl. 'Sorry mate, nothing's turned up.' I cursed. After all that effort we were going to be thwarted by a document delayed in the post. I called the shipping agency to see if there was anything they could do. It turned out that the ship had been delayed a day, so we still had a chance. Breathe … stay calm. The Carnet just had to turn up the next morning.

And it did.

Next stop East Timor: Dot on a cargo boat, me on a plane.

4

Bitter Sweet Symphony

To East Timor

I really don't like flying. I think it's that moment when you reach the top of the climb, the engines are at full thrust and you can hear them screaming as the plane climbs, reaches cruising altitude, and then *click*, the engines go ghostly silent. In that moment I feel a real sense of impending doom that has me grip the armrests at the thought of what I imagine is about to happen.

I think I'd be all right if the plane just exploded in midair; I could deal with that. No time to know it. But if the engines packed up and you had a minute of freefall as the plane careered towards the ground, I couldn't think of anything worse. Sixty seconds to reflect on things, to question whether you've done enough, been enough, seen enough. Lived enough. I say that because what if the answer to that is 'no'? Now it's too late to do anything about it. What's not been said never will be, what's not been done never will be. Your chance has gone. Though I guess this is the fear of regret. Not flying.

The plan from here was to land in Dili, the capital of East Timor, find somewhere to lay low for a week while waiting for Dot to arrive, then cross the border to West Timor. That would put us in Indonesia. All I knew about the place was that it was a huge chain of islands, mainly Muslim, each connected by ferry and the length from one end to the other easily as far as the distance from Sydney to Perth. My route was going to be a simple one. From one island to the other to the other — Timor, Flores, Sumbawa, Lombok, Bali, Java, Sumatra — until a month from now I'd hopefully make the jump across to Malaysia and begin working my way up from there to Thailand and then across through India, Pakistan, Iran etc., places still so far away I didn't bother to give them much thought. They didn't exist yet.

My focus now, though, was on East Timor, one half of an island just two hours north of Darwin. I was nervous because I'd never been anywhere in Asia before. And now I was about to land in one of its darker corners with no map or guidebook or any accommodation booked. All I'd got was the name of a hostel I'd found online and written on a scrap of paper. It wasn't ideal, but given the rush to get Dot on the boat, and me on the plane the following morning — one day over my visa — there wasn't much else I could do. Just jump in at the deep end and hope I float. On the plane I sat next to an East Timorese man who'd been on an oil-drilling course in Darwin. He was quite shocked by my plan and lack of preparation. He told me about the past troubles there and some of the things I would encounter. It didn't sound good.

And to think, on that exact same day, on the other side of the world, somewhere above the city of London, another aeroplane would be preparing to land. One of its seats would be empty, my seat, the one I would now have been sitting in had it not been for Mandy giving me the encouragement and support to do this instead. She was the one who said you can do it, that you should do it. After all I'd put her through she was still thinking of what was best for me. I sat there and wondered what she would be doing now, whether she was missing me, or, I feared, glad to be getting her lasagne off someone else.

For now the wing dipped, the seatbelt light lit, and below an island looking like the one from Jurassic Park came into view.

Mayday mayday, we're going down.

* * *

I sat on one of the plastic seats in the tiny airport terminal with my head in my hands. I had my laptop on one shoulder, my SLR camera over the other and my rucksack squeezed tightly between my knees. I pulled my cap down low. People swarmed around me, buzzing about my ear. 'Hey mister, hey mister, taxi taxi, where you from, where you go?' I heard them, but didn't dare look up, just kept my head down, wishing for the ground to open and swallow me up.

It was 7.30 a.m., I was lathered in sweat and well and truly out of my depth. It was a moment where the realisation of scale and situation hit me, and I looked around, and thought,

'What the hell am I doing, here, in this land, no clue, no whereabouts, and when my bike arrives I've got to find the road that runs across the island and follow it all the way across the world, through lands even more dangerous and hot than this one.'

A white, middle-aged woman came to my rescue. I spotted her dropping off other Europeans in the yard outside the terminal. This was my opportunity, and I took it, scooping up my things, blustering through the crowd of men still hounding me before she had time to drive away. I approached her from the rear, calling out in my meekest voice, 'Excuse me, do you know of the guesthouse in town?'

She spun around, 'Of course my dear,' and offered me a lift.

I jumped in the passenger seat of her tiny people carrier. She introduced herself as Jill, an Australian, who was out here helping kids with malnutrition. As we headed for the city, along the beaten-up main road, she explained how she'd had to remortgage her own house in order to fund the new clinic she'd just had constructed in the city. It sounded necessary. The previous day she'd carried the body of a child on the seat I was sitting in now. He had died from malnutrition. Jill talked with a weary acceptance of the world; a lone woman on a mission. She reminded me of Sigourney Weaver in *Gorillas in the Mist*.

She asked what I was doing here. I told her. She thought it sounded a dangerous idea, recounting some terrible stories from the country's past and also its present. She said I would have to be very careful and not go out after dark. I looked around. There was no chance of that. I saw animals in cages, vegetables being sold on the ground, wooden shacks, littered wastelands, and a world of short, dark-skinned men in dusty sandals and shorts. There seemed no order to any of it, only chaos. It was hot, dirty, and the roads were horrific; lorries and trucks charging about. A jungle landscape smothered the hills all around.

Finally we pulled up outside a big metal gate with barbed-wire across the top. Beneath it was a sign: 'Dili Smokehouse'. It was the name of the place I'd written on my piece of paper. 'This is it,' Jill said, as I realised the need for me to get out. I couldn't thank her enough. She gave me her business card and told me where her clinic was in case I wanted to stop by. I grabbed all my things, slammed the door on her battered minibus, turned, and walked through the gate and down the driveway to the building at the bottom. 'Welcome to East Timor,' I thought to myself.

I turned right and went through a gate. This led into a leafy courtyard, full of shade and colour. There was a bar in one corner. Behind it stood a tiny Timorese woman with a beaming smile; her name was Rita. I asked if she'd got a room, anything. I was in luck; she had just the thing, opening a door across the courtyard leading into a room painted pink, with boards across the window at the far end. It was a square-shaped room with two single beds in one corner, then two bunks and, in the far corner, another bed and a wardrobe. Seven beds in total. One of them was now mine. Ten bucks a night, US, not Australian.

I threw my gear on a top bunk, though I had to be careful

not to miss my step climbing up so high, for whenever you are in a country your government advises you not to go to, like East Timor, Pakistan and areas of other countries I would be passing through, your travel insurance is automatically null and void. This was worrying, especially given my previous track record. But there's nothing you can do. I would just have to be extra careful, not only climbing up to the top bunk, but also on the roads. Though if I'd ignored my government's advice, then so had the other people staying there.

There was Faustoe, a lively backpacker from Italy who had travelled the world and conquered every woman he'd met along the way by the sounds of things. He could talk endlessly about himself, and he did, but he was a great guy to be around, playing a guitar and making up songs about me, and about Darren, a young guy from Singapore who had come here for a holiday, through curiosity. Dressed like a badminton player, he looked awkward and out of place, but strangely nothing seemed to faze him. He talked to, and took photos of, everyone he met. Mal was even more laid back. He was a hippy from Perth, with dreadlocks, and had a job in a quarry which he didn't particularly like, but it was necessary, he conceded, to finance his love of travel.

Finally the Germans, Sven and Caroline, who were pedalling around the world on big heavy-framed pushbikes. They had already crossed South America and Australia and were now heading the same way as me back to Europe. If I was mad, then they were mental. Bags were bolted to every bit of their bikes, they carried spare wheels and across the

Australian Outback even pulled a trailer. They also had the most romantic story. They met not many weeks before Sven was due to set off on a big cycling adventure. A few weeks into it he missed Caroline so much he turned around, cycled back and waited a year until Caroline was ready to come cycling as well. And off they went, into the sunset.

The hostel was a fascinating place. At night the brothers and cousins and distant relatives of Rita, who all slept on mattresses on the floor, would sit up watching porn; they'd even do it during the day. But nobody minded, it was just part of the place's charm, which also included a grim dirty kitchen with plates and cutlery you daren't touch and a toilet block that's best not described. The place was in a real state, though homely; the Australian owner was no longer well enough to run it, leaving Rita to manage the trickle of backpackers that came through the gate.

For food we'd always go to the open-air Indian diner next door. There were rats running around your feet and you could see straight through to the filthy kitchen where the food was being slopped out. Maybe the filth added flavour, because it was good stuff, especially the dosas we had for breakfast, which we washed down with spicy chai tea. We got talking to the owner. He told us he had just paid $700 for a UK work visa off the internet but couldn't understand why the agency who issued it wouldn't now respond to his emails. None of us had the heart to tell the bloke they probably never would.

Finally, after two days lying low in the hostel, I thought it finally time to man up and face the city. I laced up my boots and dropped my penknife in my pocket. On my iPod I played *Bitter Sweet Symphony*. I was Richard Ashcroft, get the hell out of my way ... when in reality I tiptoed down the driveway, past the barbed-wire fence, until I had no choice but to step out onto the street. The pace of it hit me. The heat, the bustle, the commotion — this was Asia, and the air sang with life. Dogs running past, people shouting, the traffic in chaos — to cross the road, you just had to step out and hope they'd stop.

What struck me as I wandered further were how nice the houses would have been before they were either shot at, burned down or blown up. Some were just charred remains; others were still quite pretty. I cut through one estate, walking past a refugee camp — just a canopy of makeshift tents — and found myself down on the waterfront where the flags of foreign countries fluttered above a monument. If you ignored the stranded bottles, the pieces of blue foam, the random sandal, the driftwood and the soft drink cans, it was a beautiful beach, arching the length of a city similar in size to Darwin. At the far end of the beach a statue of Jesus was perched high up on the cliffs — a reminder that this was a Catholic country, thanks to its Portuguese colonists, who left in 1975.

I walked further, past the busy dock where Dot would finally arrive, and on to a spot where teenagers sat on the sea wall kicking it with their heels the way bored teenagers do the world over. They wore trainers and fashionable jeans. Some waved and said hello. They were friendly, welcoming; they wanted to talk but we couldn't understand one another. Women selling water would smile and the men chopping coconuts would offer me one. I was a stranger in a foreign land but I was being treated well. I still felt nervous, too conspicuous for my liking. I tripped over pavements, I nearly fell down the open drains. I kept one hand on my wallet, the other on my knife.

By the side of the road I met Richard from Australia. We chatted a while. Sweating in the heat, he told me he was here to see if he could set up a fair-trade coffee processing plant, as East Timor was currently selling raw beans to other countries, which made all the money on processing. His plan was to set up a facility so that could be done 'in-house' instead. The country sure needed the money. The buildings, the roads, the infrastructure — it was all in ruins. And yet there'd be five electrical stores on one street and brand-new scooters parked outside each and every one. Richard explained that a lot of the cash came from relatives working in Europe or America sending money home to their families. So while the country's poor, some of its people, relatively speaking, aren't so badly off.

Fascinated by the place, I borrowed a book from an English lady setting up a shop down the road. It was called *A Dirty Little War*, written by an Australian journalist who witnessed the turbulent period of 1999 first hand. This was the year in which East Timor won its independence from Indonesia, after almost twenty-five years of occupation, a period in which it's claimed as many as 100,000 people died through starvation and violence. The split was violent and bloody, thanks to the Indonesian-backed militia, and it had taken years to arrive at the modest stability I now witnessed.

It really made me think; those people chopping coconuts and hounding me to buy things, even Rita, had lived through all that. They'd seen crowds fired on by soldiers, babies having their heads battered against rocks, friends and neighbours shot and raped in front of them. I probably heard about some of it on the news at the time and perhaps, as unpleasant as it is to think, told myself that such people don't grieve like us, they have so many children they don't care so much, or somehow a gruesome death is accepted, commonplace in some parts of the world, whether it be East Timor or Africa. But I was here now, confronted by it, realising it was just the same as if a foreign army occupied Sydney and shot all the people in the CBD.

To keep the peace and help the country stand on its own two feet the United Nations were now here in force. Moving along every road and parked outside every restaurant, shop and bank, or so it seemed, were new Toyota 4x4s, painted white with the organisation's initials in blue down the side. Many of the international aid agencies were here as well, including the Red Cross and Oxfam — they, too, were in brand-new Toyotas. In fact, the Japanese manufacturer was doing such a good trade in East Timor they'd built a huge glass-fronted dealership on the road to the airport, next door to the wooden shacks in which the local people lived.

Of an evening, the staff of these organisations would drink imported beer and eat steak in the restaurants and bars they'd built along the seafront. No locals ate in them; prices were too high, the same as you'd pay in Australia. In here you'd get talking to the sons of the UN envoy, to the foreign soldiers, and to those working for the aid agencies who lived in secure compounds throughout the city, often with maids. I found out that they were all on maximum pay whenever our governments advise against visiting the country.

The cynical side of me saw this as being quite convenient, because to look at these people I would say they were all on holiday while telling us lot to stay away. Then you pick up the local magazine and read how the UN need more money for their operations around the world. Given what Jill had been prepared to do to build her clinic, I couldn't help but think if they all bought second-hand Toyotas and stopped spending all their money on piss, the money they already had might go a bit further.

But in fairness to the UN and the other agencies, there was certainly something, a presence, an unease, that I still struggle to put my finger on. Sometimes it felt like paradise, as though those UN personnel weren't needed at all. And then at other times you could understand why they were here — you sensed something, a crackle in the air, a ripple of turbulence in the fabric of the city. The locals were friendly and none approached me with any ill-intent, but when I asked them about the past or for opinions on the state of the country they turned shy. I got the impression they were being very careful about what they said, but with Indonesian informants probably still in the city it was perhaps no wonder. If you were drunk on that imported beer you probably wouldn't notice anything wrong at all. But to me it felt like a city still quietly simmering.

One day, as I was sitting in the leafy courtyard of the Dili Smokehouse minding my own business, a man with a ponytail and a thick moustache turned up. Rita said she knew him and they chatted before he made his way over to me. He was friendly, in an overly inquisitive way. He wanted to know about my camera and my laptop and my trip. He wanted to take my picture — which made me worry because, I mean, why would he? All sorts of theories ran through my mind and I withdrew from the conversation. I began to wonder if he was some kind of spy, sent to suss me out after I'd put 'journalist' on my visa application (which was true enough, because I was working on a car magazine before going back to Australia to make sandwiches for a living).

Jill, who I visited at the clinic, said I might be pulled in for interrogation as a consequence of this admission. I'd brushed that off as being too dramatic, but in the book I'd borrowed I'd read that journalists had been targeted and killed during Indonesian times. So, when the moustachioed man returned the next day and suggested I go with him up into the mountains to visit his relatives, I was genuinely scared. My mind turned to the poster of a missing Swedish backpacker on the hostel wall. He was last seen in East Timor two years ago, vanishing without trace. It made me aware of my vulnerability. I could disappear in the morning and no one would know until the emails dried up. It was for this reason my parents posted me a GPS tracker unit, allowing them to trace online my every move.

I felt at risk. Mal thought I was overreacting and said it could be the anti-malaria tablets making me paranoid. I remembered the doctor in Darwin warning me that the tablets could have that side effect, but it was so hard to tell whether it was the drugs or the realisation of where I was and the scale of what I was aiming to do that was finally catching up with me.

After all, Australia had been a long hard slog in a familiar land. I knew the culture and I understood the language. Now I was in East Timor, the toe of Asia, looking northwest up the leg of Indonesia, questioning whether I could do this. And if I was uncertain of myself at this early point, what about when I reached India, Pakistan and Iran? How would I cope in countries with reputations as fierce as those?

From this point on I would have to overcome the fear of being alone on a bike in a foreign land. I'd have to overcome the fear of not knowing how to fix my bike, of not knowing if I had enough money to finish, of not knowing how long it would take, of not knowing how I would cross Indonesia, of not planning anything in advance. There was so much I didn't know, and yet for all that I had a sense that I was on the right path, doing the right thing, in the right place.

There was no doubt or indecision, just fear, and I think that's the right way round. Fear you can face, but doubt and indecision — that's not a nice place to be. Treading water, going nowhere while your mind ties itself up in knots. I didn't have that out here, just a simple challenge, to ride as hard and as far as I could, to find out what Asia was like for myself and see if one day I would make it to England. This was my challenge now and all East Timor had done was hit me with the danger of it, the reality.

I'd met people already doing similar things and realised for the time being I came up short. Yet I'd tried the food and realised it wasn't too bad. I'd seen the roads and knew with more care I could survive. By now I also knew that such endeavours came at a price. And what you gain with one hand you lose with the other. There are consequences to a trip like this. You are forced to make a choice, to leave something or someone behind. Most of all, you are made to question yourself and confront the things you don't like most about yourself. And not all the time are you happy with how you answer.

How far would we get? I wasn't sure. The man at the Indonesian Embassy, just around the corner from the Dili Smokehouse, reckoned I wouldn't be able to take my foreign motorcycle over the border into West Timor. He told me this the day I went to collect my tourist visa. I argued with him, presenting my Carnet and telling him of the other couple on the postie who'd passed this way six months before. But he was adamant; Dot would not be able to enter Indonesia. And if that was the case the only way around would be to put her on a boat *back* to Darwin, then another one to Singapore, and fly there myself. No way could I have afforded that. But I remained optimistic, racing down to the Dili docks the day Dot's boat finally arrived, intent on finding out for myself whether she could cross the Indonesian border or not. I would soon find out.

5

Angels and Demons

Dili Onwards

It had cost me $300 to ship Dot from Darwin to East Timor, a simple process in Australia. I just took her down to the docks, had her weighed and measured, then went into the office to pay. But retrieving her at the other end in Dili was a different matter. First I had to go to the docks to have my Carnet stamped, taking two days because the staff work to what's locally known as 'banana time', for the way it bends. After that it was to the office of the shipping agency in the centre of town to pay the Customs fees and then back to the docks with the receipt. I was then hastily bundled into a taxi and driven beyond the outskirts of town. We came to a stop at the gates of a dusty yard stacked high with big metal cargo containers.

'No way can Dot be here,' I thought, as I walked through the yard, the jungle pushing up against the perimeter fence, giving my documents to a man who with a team of labourers led me down to the third container on the left, the one with the red door — they all had red doors. When they opened it I peered inside and all I could see were pallets of food. I felt deflated, looking at the team of men in their blue and yellow overalls and wondering if this was the right one. With that a forklift truck was summoned and slowly the men began to drag the pallets out: two pallets, three, four, a flash of red, then a gleam of headlight. Well blow me down, Dorothy was in there after all.

The labourers wheeled her out into the sunlight. It was good to see her again. She'd managed to survive the seven days at sea, not to mention the gruelling ride across the Outback, completely intact. I dread to imagine my mood had it been Doris rolling out of that metal container with her oil leak and milk crate strapped on the back. I would have been dubious. To try and ensure Dot didn't fall victim to the same fate, my intention was to change her oil every 1500 kilometres and keep her frequently serviced. I would have to be careful, though; counterfeit oil is a common problem in Asia, and it's difficult to tell apart from the real thing, until your bike comes to a noisy halt.

This then was going to be the start of a steep learning curve. From here on in, I would have to figure out the simple things like food and fuel and places to stay. Navigating my way would also be different now the people I asked no longer spoke English. The flow of traffic I would also have to fathom, realising that out here villagers build their own speed traps in the form of ditches across the road which you might not see until you hit them. Having people pass me on bikes wearing no crash helmets was also strange, that they were joined by two kids and a wife on the same saddle was also new. Other questions: where will I find genuine oil for Dot, where will I pump her tyres up, what do I do if I break down or get into trouble?

And then changing money, how much would I need to carry, where was the next cash machine, can I change money over the border or before it? How will I be welcomed riding through, as friend or enemy? Might I be robbed, is it wise that I reveal my camera, where do I wee, where do I buy toilet rolls, and if I'm sick where do I go because hospitals are rare? All the aspects of life I'd taken for granted had to be re-evaluated and learnt again on the road in the next few weeks.

I spent a few days riding around Dili — just getting used to the roads — even heading out with Mal, Faustoe and Darren, who rented scooters from a petrol station near the hostel. They were better times, riding as a group, on the road around the island, despite Mal falling off and injuring himself. Then it was back alone, making haste along the coastal road in the direction of the border with West Timor. Houses were built in the sand on the beaches, kids on their way to school high-fived me as I passed. But for the troubles, the island really was beautiful. Then I spotted a sign for the village of Maliani. It was near there that five Australian journalists were executed as the Indonesians invaded in 1975.

This was a sobering reminder that, whether or not I'd imagined the threat of the moustachioed man, the events of that year were real. People had died and for the next twenty-five years they continued to do so. The Indonesians had now been removed from the eastern half of the island; the UN and all their white trucks were there to ensure they didn't return. But very soon I would be crossing into the country from which the murderers and rapists had come. There I would have no protection. I would be on my own. Just the road. And a penknife in my pocket.

I should, then, have been scared to enter West Timor (of course the man at the embassy had been wrong), yet crossing the border was like putting heavy bags down after a trip to the supermarket. You know, when you've carried them up the drive and through the door and the handles are hurting your hand and you can't wait to get to the kitchen so you can at last rest them on the floor and shake the numbness from your hand. That's what I felt leaving East Timor. As though I'd just let go of the baggage. I waved at every West Timorese person I saw. I stopped for photos. Bought petrol from the roadside in little glass bottles. I felt great; the paranoia was lifting. Then I got to Atambua, where I'd spend the first night, and it struck again like a brick.

Riding into town, a man on a moped started following me. I tried to shake him off through the back streets, but when I stumbled upon a hotel he pulled up right behind me. I wanted to tell him to clear off, but I never have been one for confrontation. Just let it slide, don't antagonise; but as he hovered around and joked in his own language with the people standing nearby I felt extremely vulnerable. For all I might have said about the UN, this was the town where three of their staff were murdered in 2000. It was the town where the Indonesian militia had fled to after East Timor won its independence. And it gave off that vibe. I asked him his name; it was Adi. I wrote his motorcycle's registration number on the back of my hand and walked into reception.

I was given a room around the back. It had no sink or shower but I could leave Dot near the door. I talked to a French couple on their patio across the courtyard. They were in their fifties, travelling through to East Timor by local bus. That evening I sat and shared a cup of tea on their balcony, copying some of the maps in their travel guide into my diary and writing down the names of the major towns so that I would at least have places to aim for. Travelling without such things isn't as big a deal as it sounds. Islands generally only have one road across them. I figured if I stuck to that main road I couldn't really go wrong.

Then another strange thing happened. One of the guards from the earlier border crossing checked into a room across the courtyard. I asked him what he was doing there. He said he was staying at the hotel because the water pipes had burst at his own house. I didn't believe it. Most of these houses don't even have running water. It was too much of a coincidence for my liking. The moustachioed man, Adi, and now him — this was getting worrying. I dragged the mattress close to the window, chained Dot to the fence outside (having first tried to squeeze her through the door) and balanced a beer bottle on her footrest as a crude booby-trap. If the bottle were to fall in the night I was ready armed with the hammer and penknife I kept on the pillow.

Of course, the next morning everything was fine. Dot was still there, nothing touched. Over breakfast, the French couple gave me some different anti-malaria tablets so I could get off the Lariam. Was it that making me paranoid, or did I have a genuine reason to be suspicious? The puzzle was solved later that morning when I stopped to buy a sim card for my phone in a shop on the outskirts of town. I was at the counter paying when suddenly Adi walked in, clear as day, with his head down so I wouldn't recognise him. 'Are you following me?' I asked. He shook his head, but it seemed too much of a coincidence to me. I reasoned he must have watched me leave the hotel and followed me to the phone shop. He was on a different bike to the one he'd used last night; I checked the rego number against the one still on my hand.

I blustered past him, threw on the helmet, fired Dot into life and for the next eight hours just rode, and rode and rode, all the way to Kupang on the island's western tip, where we hoped to catch a ferry to the next island that same day. I kept expecting to see Adi approaching fast on his moped, or pulling up for petrol alongside, still grinning, still following me. I looked for people using their mobile phones by the side of the road; I figured they might be communicating with him. It was like travelling with a dark shadow that day. I was scared, genuinely believing that something bad was going to happen — a black dog barking at my heels. All I hoped was that I'd make the ferry in Kupang before it ever caught me.

Disaster. The ferry that day had already sailed. Not only that, but I'd have to wait two weeks for the next one. I had to ask again. 'Two weeks, yeah I thought that's what you said.' I was devastated by this. I just wanted to leave. I kept looking behind me. I kept spotting Adi, he was everywhere. On every motorbike, at every food stall. I'd been working on the assumption that the local ferries were running every day and that I didn't need to plan such things. But with the weather too rough for the smaller boats, it was only the bigger fortnightly ferry that was still sailing. I was angry with myself for not finding this out sooner. I could have done some research in Dili, I could have known this before setting off, but no, I'd stuck to my belief that there was no hardship in making it up as I went along, and now I'd come seriously unstuck.

And that wasn't the only problem. In my blind ambition, or arrogance, I'd thought it not necessary to apply for a two-month Indonesian visa and settled for a one-month visa instead. People more experienced had told me that one month wouldn't be long enough to ride across the country, especially on Dot. But I'd not listened, remembering how much I'd enjoyed the thrill of the 'chase' across the Outback, and thought it would be nice to have that sense of urgency again. A month would be plenty. But now I wouldn't have a month, I would have two weeks, to ride six islands, along terrible roads, catching ferries and covering a distance of at least 4000 kilometres, if not 5000. And the worst part about it was that there was nothing I could do. Only wait.

I checked into a cheap hotel by the waterfront and had a walk around the city that evening. Kupang was the same size as Dili and had the same rundown look about it. But there were no white 4x4s, or UN soldiers. No bullet holes in the buildings or refugee camps in the streets. Though in some ways Kupang was worse off for it. In Dili you sensed the previous pain; it had that haunted feeling, people were reserved and silently proud, they were survivors. Here in the West there was much more confidence, more bravado. You could tell they'd been the island's dominant half. And so instead of a smile and a wave, the children would bark 'Hey mister' to get your attention and then laugh when you gave it. I felt they were taunting me and I didn't like it.

This, though, was a good time for me and Mandy to catch up. There was an internet café from which I could email her, and with a local sim card we could even speak on the phone. Of course it wasn't easy, especially now the dust had settled and we'd both had time to reflect on things. Now we had the discussions we should have had in the days before I left, about the future and stuff. Such things were tough, and uncomfortable, though it was just nice to chat and to catch up and cast some bow ropes between us as we drifted further and further apart. There'd been a great deal of optimism the day I'd set off and, although it had waned, it was still there; we'd been through too much for it not to. And to think this all began at speed-dating.

I often think how odd it is that one moment in life can have such a profound impact on the rest of it. It's almost as if your life is a bullet, fired from a gun and shooting dead straight until it takes a ricochet on an old watering can and goes pinging off in an entirely different direction. The man in the corner drops down dead, the mongrel you were aiming for is still grinning. Whether they are the people we meet or the things we see or experience, many millions of life's moments pass us by with virtually no effect on us at all, at least not in any significant way. And then along comes a few minutes that can change everything.

I'd given some thought to this on my last night in Darwin as I watched a group of homeless men collect food from a charity van down at the park. I'd thought, here I was on this adventure; I didn't have much money, but hopefully enough. I had a family supporting me and friends wishing me well. And then here was this group of men: no home, no family, no food of their own, some as young as twenty. For me it was a strange form of dating that had led me to Darwin that night. But what about these guys, what was their 'moment' that brought them here? Was it abuse, drugs, alcohol, mental illness, like we often suspect, or was one of their 'moments' simply a bad one and it all went downhill from there? I reasoned that entirely possible. Like the homeless guy I used to serve at the café, once a successful lawyer until his mind went blank. It made me realise how close we all are to sitting in a park, waiting to be fed.

After a week, the weather calmed and the man in the bar over the road told me there was a local ferry sailing that very day. This was great news, meaning I'd have three weeks to ride the length of Indonesia, not two. And that was a huge difference; I figured I could do it in that time without having to get an extension in Bali which I'd been told I could get. With the ferry sailing in just a few hours, I packed up my gear as fast as I possibly could, paid my bill for the hotel, apologised to the owner for not being able to attend his father's funeral later that day (which I'd been invited to), and made great haste to the docks, where at the end of a long wooden rickety pier a rusting boat was waiting. I bought a ticket, paid the police their bribe and rolled onboard. Goodbye Timor, I shall miss you, but not very much.

6

Soup Bowl

Leaving Timor

The boat was going to take eighteen hours and sail through the night. It was two decks high, about the size of your local swimming pool and once painted white but now riddled with rust. I'd parked to the left of the vehicle deck at the end of a line of brand-new scooters. The only other vehicle onboard was a battered truck in the middle with all sorts of groceries packed on top. In front of that were a dozen cages of clucking chickens, all scrawny and part-feathered. I saw passengers going up a set of steps to what I can only imagine was a seating area, but keen to keep an eye on Dot I thought it better to stay on the lower deck, leaning over the side, watching Timor slowly disappear from view.

The other passengers loved having a foreign man with a motorbike onboard. Some were curious for five minutes, others for ten, but there was one man who was curious all night. I didn't trust him. Very quickly you learn who to trust and who not to. You might sometimes be wrong but it's a natural thing you do. And I didn't trust him. He was stocky, and his eyes were shifty, dark with menace. Sometimes he would come and lean on Dot's handlebars and smoke a cigarette, not saying a word. He'd disappear for ten minutes, then come back and do it again. Eventually I asked what he wanted and he just shrugged. I was intimidated by him and made a note to avoid him when we reached the other end.

My other companion that night was a woman scrunched up beneath a blanket sleeping against the wheel of the truck. She must have had the flu, because every minute or so she would clear her lungs of green sticky phlegm and spit it across the deck, or blow it through her nose onto her fingers, which she would then flick. Where it landed, God knows. It went on through the night. Sinus Night. The whole deck covered in her snot. I lay between Dot and a row of other scooters on a wicker mat I bought for a dollar, being bothered by the man, being disgusted by the woman, trying to get some sleep. The floor was cold hard steel.

At the Flores dock the next morning, a crowd of local sellers jumped the boat before it'd even landed, like pirates swinging on the end of a rope. I hopped on Dot, made sure everything was bolted down and secure, buckled up the helmet and wobbled through the crowd of people that darted towards me with goods to sell. I left them behind and headed to the main town of Ende, a few kilometres from the port, where I planned on staying the night. Immediately I got a bad vibe; it was a dusty port town, with gangs of youths sitting around on street corners, watching me pass. In the street, looking for a hotel, I met a Frenchman working for a charity who warned me to be careful. 'Don't trust anyone,' he said. On that advice I thought better of hanging around and finding the hotel, making haste for the road out of town instead. I didn't know where I was heading, only west, in the direction of the setting sun.

This felt like real adventure now, roaming through the wilderness of a very foreign land with no knowledge or faith in anything around us. I still had no map, no guidebook, no clue where I was going to stay that night. I was totally exposed and vulnerable. And that unnerved me. But it was like standing at the entrance of a bleak black wood, looking in at the gnarly trees that scared us just by being in their shade let alone walking amongst them. We'd be inclined to turn back, go around, but we couldn't, we had no choice but to enter.

Though it's funny; as I rode away from the port that day, an alien road curling out in front of me, I thought back to those Aboriginal kids in the Australian Outback, the ones I'd backed away from like a coward. Of course I'd not been in any real danger; it was just my mind tricking me into thinking there was. It then dawned on me that I was showing that exact same irrational behaviour here in Indonesia, with everyone — the whole population — and that was stupid, because I was the odd one out now, and if I was to run away from everyone who looked and acted differently in this part of the world, then I'd never stop running until I fell into Europe. And I couldn't possibly do that. Well, I could, but that would be senseless.

PENANG
CAMERON HIGHLANDS
MALAYSIA
MEDAN
SARAWAK
BORNEO
SUMATRA
INDONESIA
JAVA
LOMBOK
FLORES
BALI
SUMBAWA
DILI
WEST TIMOR
KUPANG
EAST TIMOR
TIME IN EAST TIMOR: 2 WEEKS
TIME IN INDONESIA: 4 WEEKS
TOTAL DISTANCE COVERED: 6000KMS
① DILI - WAITING 2 WEEKS
② KUPANG - WAITING 8 DAYS FOR FERRY
③ MET ELIZABETH
④ SPENT 3 DAYS ON BALI
⑤ HIT BUS
⑥ MET BIGZONERS
⑦ CAMPED WILD FOR FIRST TIME
⑧ VISITED SCHOOL
⑨ FERRY OUT OF BELAWAN, MALACCA

It helped that Flores was beautiful, an island of peppermint Toblerone chocolate chunks rising out of the sea, huge banana leaves hiding most traces of humanity; it looked like a green blanket had been chucked over a collection of road cones. The road weaved between them, offering stunning views of watery coves pricked by tiny specks of villages just like those I'd seen in East Timor, with their smiling children and wooden houses. People walked barefoot or in sandals, they wore shorts and T-shirts from Adidas or Reebok or a football club in England. They were dark skinned, short, and seemingly very happy. I didn't see any cars, only motorbikes, usually parked outside little wooden hut-shops where I'd stop to buy a bottle of water and a packet of biscuits. I lived on biscuits now.

More often that not, one of the villagers would speak a little English, just a few words. But if they didn't, I'd say, 'Australia', and then 'Sumbawa, Lombok, Bali, Malaysia,' so they could grasp where I came from and where I was going. If I had a pen and paper handy I'd write down distances and show them the calendar on my signal-less phone so they could see how long I had been on the road. I'd tell them my name was John because they couldn't pronounce Nathan — Nay-tan, Nat-an, May-fen. I reasoned it better for everyone to speak no words of the other language at all, rather than a few. That way people are under no illusions about who they're conversing with — a foreign idiot who knows nothing — and that simplifies things. Then it was back to the steep, winding hills.

Still no clue where I was going to sleep that night, I just kept riding, through the rain, hoping something would turn up. And finally it did, a town buried in the bottom of a valley, surrounded by thick forest. We looked down on it from our vantage point up in the sky with the rainclouds. It was beautiful, a sprawl of wooden houses and huts with bulbs twinkling in the darkening light. Lush green vegetation shrouded it from every side; it was like a hidden civilisation, one that didn't want to be found but we just had, drifting down the hill and into its centre. A couple of small tourist hotels stood on either side of the road, restaurants too. All was calm and peaceful, and tourists were unpacking their rucksacks from 4x4s out front. This was a sight I never for a minute thought I'd see on Flores. I thought we were alone, and it was a relief to see that we were not.

Checking into the hotel I took a room on the first floor. I threw my things on the bed, sat down on the stool, looked in the mirror, rubbed my eyes with my hands, let out a big sigh. It was only a day ago that I'd left West Timor in a hurry. So little time had passed since then, yet so much had happened. Ferry, spitting bitch, shifty eyes, marauding 'Hey misters', my realisation that it's not all that bad. I ate dinner that night with a group of backpackers on a guided tour from Bali, now only three islands away. That was nice. They were so happy and relaxed, on holiday with the hope of seeing the volcanic Kelimutu lakes and doing some diving off one of the great beaches I'd no doubt raced past in blind panic. Their calmness and sense of confidence compared to mine led me to conclude that mood is entirely a response to circumstance, and not location.

I say that because while they were still sinking beers in the restaurant and having a laugh, I went back to the room and had a little cry. I don't know, I guess I felt swamped by things, as though I'd got nothing left to give and was tired of being continuously on edge. I wasn't having fun. Which is stupid because I was in a gorgeous part of the world on a motorbike not having to work: what could be so bad about that? I suppose the joy of solitude I talked about so fondly in the Outback had now been replaced by loneliness.

I thought of Mandy. She was now two hours behind. That would mean she was not long home from work. She might have driven or she might have used her pushbike. Dinner would be on, a stir-fry or a chicken wrap. While it was cooking she might be hanging out the washing or talking to her housemates in the back garden. Being a teacher she might have some marking to do or some lessons to plan. She'd do this in her bedroom, lying on her bed, with a glass of wine perhaps, maybe with the telly on. Outside it would be sunny and bright. Traffic would be calming. Sydney would be settling down for the night. Just as she would be doing in her bedroom now. I wished I was there. To massage her back and stroke her hair. Make her tea if she fancied one. Listen to her snore as she drifted off. If only we could live in the world nostalgia creates. If only that world existed.

Next day, back on the road, with a twelve-hour ride to the port town of Labuanbajo at the very western tip of Flores. This was better, a single destination at the end of a very long road with nothing to do but keep the throttle at the stop. You didn't have to make any decisions or think too hard, just flick your mind to neutral and try and absorb the gorgeous green world as it came howling at you. No need for a map, just follow the road, the houses along it creating a wood-shack canyon with kids and goats darting out and cheering as me and Dot rode past with a wave.

Locals would try and race us. They'd come careering past, no helmets, just T-shirts and shorts, their feet in thongs and their toes pointing outwards with their knees tucked right in. Racing style. Around the corners they'd ride flat out, handlebars almost grinding grooves in the tarmac and the family on the back not even caring to scream. Without government regulation and the police to enforce it, they seemed to have found a neat position between moderation and excess, and looked happy in it.

What I liked most was the way time seemed to slow down when you made eye contact with the people in the villages as you passed. I might be doing fifty kilometres per hour, but still, I would look at the old man sitting in the shade and he would look at me, and in that split-second it felt like we almost engaged in conversation. It was all facial expressions and the reactions to them, the pair of us able to convey so much about who we were and what we were thinking, almost to the point at which you felt you could predict what type of person they were, whether they were gentle or violent, whether they were happy to see you or otherwise. Time would once again speed back up and on you'd go to the next person, where you'd do the same thing all over again. I must have met a thousand people a day that way.

Finally, after a long day in the saddle, me and Dot made it to Labuanbajo, a little port town overlooking a lovely clear blue bay. Along the dug-up-and-dirty main street, travellers with backpacks tried to find men with boats willing to take them to see nearby Komodo Island, home to the famous dragons. They weren't really dragons, just big lizards, but if they called them that fewer people would go. I wanted to go myself, but the tight schedule wouldn't allow the day it would take to get there and back. Instead I stayed that night in the town and caught the first ferry out of there next morning.

For the next few days I rode and caught ferries from noon until sunset. I stayed in whatever place I could find, ate at roadside stalls, and wrote the name of the next town on my hand and showed it to locals, who almost always pointed me the right way. It was a better time, and I got to see Indonesian life through all stages of the day. First thing in the morning I'd see villagers stretch and yawn as they got out of bed. I saw mothers cooking breakfast and serving it up on big wooden tables outside. Children in uniform would walk along the side of the road to school, the call to prayer would sound, and then people would go to work, in the rice fields or in the tiny wooden hut-shops that stood in front of many of their houses.

The full heat of the sun would then cook the day. Around lunchtime the families, especially the men, would sit under wicker huts, just talking, snoozing, losing, playing card games. If this were Spain, they'd be having a siesta. And then the late afternoon would come, more work would be done, children would return home and play badminton in the dirt outside their houses before eating dinner around that table again. Mother and father, brothers and sisters, aunts and uncles, all digging in. Then the boys would take girls out on scooters and come roaring past me and Dorothy as we drifted through, fascinated by the life people lived out here.

Somewhere in the middle of Sumbawa I stopped in a town with a military base to buy a map. I quite liked the idea of having one now, if only to acknowledge the sights I was missing in my haste to cross the islands before *this* visa expired. At a small stationery store I was told by the man that he didn't have any maps, but his sister-in-law, who was Australian, might be able to help. I thought to myself, 'There can't really be an Australian out here, we're too far off the beaten track.' But I followed him anyway, weaving down the back alleys on our motorbikes, eventually pulling up outside a cute little house, where sure enough, inside was a true-blue Australian, Elizabeth, from Melbourne.

She emerged from the house wearing a long red traditional Indonesian dress and told me a lovely story about the man she'd met in Bali and later wed. And now she lived here, in a world I thought looked quite lonely, a prison perhaps. But she seemed happy, with new family around her and satellite television. She said Bali was less than a day's ride away and that I wouldn't need a map. We sat and drank tea and talked about the country we both missed. I think we both enjoyed the brief companionship that afternoon. Two strangers in a foreign land. 'Nice to meet you,' I said as I waved goodbye and made my way back through the alleys and rejoined the main road. We crossed Sumbawa in a day and a half; just follow your nose.

The ferry to Bali only took a few hours, cost a couple of bucks and continued a trend of gradual refinement the closer I got to Java. That first night in Bali I stayed in a guesthouse overlooking the beach before heading to the main town of Kuta the next morning. Surf shops and nightclubs everywhere. The usual international fast-food chains all in a line. I rode around a while, bought some fake designer sunglasses, had a chat with some guys in the Aussie pub and took some pictures of the beach, which I was disappointed to find was dirty and swarming with people trying to sell you something. The poor girls in their bikinis were a magnet for all sorts of creeps. I turned and said to Dorothy, 'Let's go girl, this isn't the place for us.'

Someone had told me about Ubud, a town at the very heart of Bali with a pace apparently much calmer than Kuta. It sounded perfect, so we headed there, working slowly through the densely populated southern end of the island, wading through the thick traffic and out along industrial roads until I turned down a side street and found myself in a different world. There were ancient temples here, Buddhists in orange robes, arts and crafts stores, and wild monkeys roaming the peaceful leafy streets. I only had a couple of weeks to ride a distance of around 4000 kilometres, across Java and Sumatra, along terrible roads to the very tip of Indonesia. It was going to be a great challenge. But a month on from my arrival in East Timor, I felt a few days' recuperation in a place like this would do me good.

A couple of Yankee backpackers I met in the street directed me to a guesthouse a short ride out of town. It was only a small place, family owned, surrounded by rice fields cascading down the hill like a set of steps. The sky was blue, the air was warm, the coffee, as it always is in Indonesia, was strong. I sat on the veranda looking out at the view; not a sound. No gears to change, no trucks to avoid or ferries to race for. Just my coffee to drink and the day to relax. I took a hot shower, the first I'd had in a long time, as all those between here and Darwin had been ladles of cold water, poured over my head, and refilled from a murky 'bath' found in the corner of all Indonesian bathrooms. Of course there'd been no toilet paper either; eat with your right, wipe with your left.

This was better. A lazy few days, sauntering down into town to sit in a café and drink ginger tea while using my laptop to upload my photos to Facebook. I'd order some food, sit for a few hours, talk to other people who came in, or head off and explore. I rode Dot up to the Agung volcano, circling its rim before dropping down into its black rock crater. I rode around it for fun. On the way back I got stopped by the police and asked to produce my international driving licence. They caught out many foreigners this way. Mine was back at the hotel so I was fined almost ten bucks. The next day I was pulled over again, this time for running a red light, which I think the policeman had just made up because I didn't see one. He said I could either go to court or pay him a fine (a full day's budget). I offered him half of that, which he pocketed before riding away.

Perhaps I'm being naive, but this really annoyed me, and seemed to represent a general attitude towards tourists on the island. Every time I stopped to take a photograph or visit one of the Buddhist temples I would be surrounded by kids and old men trying to flog postcards or naff wooden statues, and they would not leave me alone until I rode off. I could see the desperation in their eyes, and their sadness. In a place like East Timor the kids all seemed so happy, like I say, lining up by the roadside just to tag my hand as I rode past. They never asked for anything. They were simply curious. Here some of the people bordered on the ruthless.

Then I thought what it must have been like as a Balinese, watching the tourism industry grow, becoming dependent on it for income, borrowing money to build shops and restaurants and hotels, riding the financial wave that one day came crashing down when the terrorist bombs of 2002 and 2005 went off. Tourists gone. Empty shops and hotels. Debt still to be paid. Families still to be raised. Screw the tourists that do still come for all they've got. I could understand it completely; it's not their fault, but it's not ours either. I guess it's just one of those inevitable things, the outcome of us wanting to spend money and them wanting to earn it. I just hope the same doesn't happen to a place like East Timor.

Though, if there's one memory that will always stick with me from Bali it's that of the food I ate the day I made my way to the ferry to Java. It was a dish called *bakso*, something I'd eaten before so I knew it to be a soup dish, with noodles and congealed balls of chicken floating on the surface. You'd buy it from men pushing little wooden carts down the road. They'd make it fresh and drizzle in all sorts of spices and bits of chopped herbs to give it a kick. It was dirt cheap. But the one I had this day featured a special ingredient. It was long and thin and a grey colour. I thought what the hell and nodded my head. With that the man took out his scissors and 'snip snip snip', cut the long dangly thing into the soup. It fell like little tubes of pasta into the bowl. I later learnt it was intestine.

7

Brotherhood

Java

The rest of the journey through Indonesia was a time of lonely highways and strange encounters. We had to ride harder and longer than we had ever ridden before. We had more ground to cover, less time to do it in, and on roads more treacherous than any we'd encountered so far. Those across Java were dense with trucks and other heavy traffic; those across Sumatra were remote and in a terrible state of repair. Along them we had accidents and crashes, we bent things, lost things, taught English at a school, climbed a temple, pitched a tent in the wild, and by the end of it had the biggest battle of them all trying to find a way of leaving it all behind.

It began with a bus heading straight for us. I don't know where my mind was or what I was thinking at the time, but I'd pulled out to overtake a Toyota people carrier on a blind bend and left myself nowhere to go when the bus came flying around it. I was doing at least seventy, he must have been doing the same and it was one of those moments when you see your life flash before your very eyes. All I could do was swing in as close as possible to the Toyota I was overtaking on my left and hold on tight.

BANG.

We miss a head-on impact by millimetres, the front end of the bus skimming Dot's headlight and tearing past my shoulder until it wallops into the right-hand side pannier, flinging us hard into the side of the Toyota; my left shoulder and Dot's left pannier rack bear the brunt of the impact. For a split second, as the two vehicles pass in opposite directions, we crash down the sides of both vehicles, sandwiched between them, still travelling at least sixty kilometres per hour, lucky not to go down because if we had we'd have been torn in two. All I could do was hold on tight until we blasted out the other side. I stopped a little later and inspected the damage. Both of Dot's pannier racks were bent and the welds broken. Paint from both vehicles was scuffed along our flanks.

I often wondered what would happen if I ever fell off or had a bad accident. Middle of Indonesia, a foreigner on a motorbike all alone; I didn't doubt for a minute that someone would stop and help me or at least pick up what had fallen off, but then what happens in a country where you can't always count on a nearby hospital or a speedy ambulance? And what of Dot — what would happen to her? And what of my parents, getting the call that their son has been smeared across the road in a foreign land?

We were lucky that day, but it was the shape of things to come. Over the next few days I fell off three times, got stranded down a ditch when it rained, lost my favourite hat, and got chased by the police for running a red light, which I was guilty of this time. I heard the police whistle and thought about stopping, but then remembered their rogue colleagues in Bali. And so I thought bum to you and opened the throttle and led them a merry dance across the rural roads of Java. I kept looking in my mirror for flashing blue lights, but they never came. Dot was too fast. Well, more likely, they couldn't be bothered to chase us.

Finding places to stay was always tricky on this leg of the journey, this being a road less travelled. The hotels were always for locals, in small towns, with no one who spoke English. It was always dark, and often raining, when I arrived. The owner would sign me into his huge book, taking my passport and visa details in case the police checked up, or came looking for deaf foreign bikers. I'd then be shown to a grotty room, where all night I could hear people coming and going, doors banging, men and women too. I think most of those places were really brothels. One place wouldn't have me because I was foreign; another asked if I wanted a lady sent to my room. 'No thanks,' I said, 'I'll take care of myself tonight.'

That's why I was glad when finally, after more than two months on the road, I felt confident enough to use my tent. Of course there are no campsites in Indonesia, and barely anywhere to put one up because there are so many houses built single-file alongside the road, but one evening, feeling brave, I found a dirt track that ran out of sight to an abandoned rain shelter in the corner of a field. When no one was looking I darted down the track and lay Dot on her side beneath the shelter and covered her with branches. I sat listening to the traffic passing by on the road. The sun was setting over the fields. I didn't have any food, or a stove, or a torch, or a pillow, or a roll mat after I'd thrown mine away in Darwin — just a bottle of water and a bag of chewy sweets.

Then the storm came.

With the rain thrashing down and the lightning tearing through the sky, I crawled into my tent, used my jumper as a pillow and gripped the knife. I had no internet, no telephone, even the battery on the tracker was dead, and my watch was in Australia. No one in the world knew where we were. Just me and Dot, beneath a canopy, in a remote Indonesian field watching the sky charge and flicker overhead. More rain fell. The smell was so sweet I wish I could have bottled it up to sprinkle on this page. You could say I was doing this to save money, but really, deep down, I was enjoying this moment of isolation, of being shut off from the world. And my responsibility to it. Nothing could find me out here. Not even my mistakes. Instead I performed cartwheels in the rain.

And to think I used to be scared of the dark. Not many weeks before, me and Mandy had gone camping to a spot just north of Sydney. It was a national park with a place to put your tent right down by the river. The car was parked a five-minute walk away down a lane with woods on either side. I had to go and get something from it one night. I ran the whole way there, and back again. I thought any minute something's going to come out from the woods and get me. 'You big pussy,' she said when I got back to the tent. It was true, I was. And yet strangely, a couple of months later, I was camping out alone in the Indonesian woods. Maybe now I was the monster giving other people a fright as they walked past to get something from their car.

I didn't get much sleep that night, even after the rain had stopped. Every noise I heard I would sit up, feel for my knife and peek outside to make sure there was nobody about. I dread to think what I would have done if there had been a face or a shadow. Near damn shit myself I suspect. But when I knew there was nothing but the night outside I would lie back down and drift off to sleep, waking as soon as the first rays of light scratched the tent and made my eyes dazzle. Opening the tent zip and stepping out into the wilds of Indonesia was a great feeling. And part of it was realising that I carried with me everything I needed to survive. After this night I felt I could turn to the wilderness whenever I needed a bed.

For breakfast I would stop at the little wooden shacks by the roadside for a blazingly strong coffee and whatever the woman happened to have in the pot. I would bring my diary inside with me and take the opportunity to write about that night's camping, or my worries, and concerns, and thoughts; I soon filled the book, hoping for clarity to spring up from the page. As I did so, curious locals would slowly come over, seating themselves at the same table as we all tried to communicate; but smiles and laughter — they are the two things that seemed to work best. And in a sense you get more out of the conversation this way, really having to focus to get your point across. To help, I'd use the secondhand Lonely Planet guide I'd bought in Bali — a 1995 edition with most of the listed hotels now closed — pointing out Sydney and London in relation to Indonesia, and my route across their islands. Then goodbye, and back to the road.

Riding at such a pace, doing fourteen hours a day, not stopping to see the tourist sights, just riding and riding against a deadline, there's a worry that you won't actually see or experience anything of the countries that you're passing through. But I was so focused, so alert, that I don't think I missed a thing. And I did make time when I thought it worthwhile. In one village, while eating lunch at a small stall, I was approached by a young student and asked if I could give a talk at his school, which was just around the corner. I spent three hours speaking to various classes and had lunch with the headmistress, who told me I was the first passing foreigner to accept an invitation. Perhaps that's why I was mugged like David Beckham, by the girls in white veils. They took my photo and giggled, even if I did, or because I did, look and smell like shit.

On stopping for fuel I also met an Indonesian biker gang called the BigZoners. I was coming out of the toilet wiping my hands on my trousers when I looked up and saw a dozen bikers gathered around Dot. It unnerved me; I wondered what they might want, until I realised they were only curious, and not like a gang of Hells Angels at all. In fact, they were more like university students on a motorcycle field trip who'd all agreed to wear matching black leathers. Their bikes were the biggest you could buy in Indonesia at 250cc, and fitted with homemade switchboards that operated sirens and flashing lights, even fake police stickers. They were organised. Sharp, smart, and clearly wealthier than most of the other islanders I'd met.

They made a fuss of me, and invited me over the road for a coffee. I thought, why not, and around a little table we all gathered, a stack of helmets beside us, everyone leaning in to hear about where I'd come from and where I was heading. We ate deep-fried snacks and drank more coffee. It was now midday. I had to get going, but then they asked me if I wanted to ride with them to their friend's house a few hours away. They were stopping there that night and meeting up with a load of other bike gangs that evening. I was welcome to stay with them and carry on the next morning. Tough call; I needed to ride, but I thought it can't be too often that you get to ride with an Indonesian bike gang, their motto: 'Keep Brotherhood Til Die'. So I nodded my head and said that would be nice.

I was told to go in the middle, with five bikes in front of me and five behind. I expected them to fly fast and have me and Dot pedal hard to keep up, especially given their power. But they were a bunch of dawdlers, taking it steady and sensible, with a real formality to the way the group rode. But it was nice to be riding at a pace where I didn't have to race; I just relaxed and let Dot have a bit of a coast. I must confess to feeling a little embarrassed as they fired up their sirens and forced other vehicles to pull over and let us pass, as though I was a VIP. Some of these road users were okay and smiled, but others looked annoyed, one even gave us the finger, and that made me feel very conspicuous after such a long time doing my best to blend in.

The best part was the pothole avoidance system. I'd been talked through it by Roda Dua, who was in the lead. Basically he would stick a leg out when he was swerving in that direction to miss a crater in the road. As soon as he did that, the man behind had to do the same, and back the signal was expected to flow, like a motorised Mexican wave, until all eleven bikes were safely around the pothole or other divot. It worked perfectly at first, the line of bikes moving like a snake between the various ruts, but then the road got so bad that both my feet were off the pegs, so when I did finally hit a pothole it was my bollocks that took the impact as they slapped against the petrol tank like balls against a bat. I gave up after a while and picked my own way through.

When we arrived at their friend's house we all stripped off our helmets and riding gear and flopped on the sofa and on the floor, all taking it in turns to have cold-water showers and emerge much cleaner and sweeter. We were fed, and then fed some more. A stall pulled up outside selling satay chicken and so we were fed again. That evening, we all rolled into town, where thousands of other bikers were out in their various gangs, all with their own names and emblems. I'd never seen anything quite like it; we took over the city. The noise was immense. On the insistence of Roda Dua, I'd left Dot back at the house and rode pillion with him, taking photos from the back of the bike. We ate again at a noodle stall and landed home at midnight.

The next morning they made the two of us honorary members of the gang. We would be the founding members of the English Chapter, our membership number, thirty-three, my old race number back when I motocrossed as a kid. The two digits were stickered to a metal plaque that was bolted to the back of Dot. That was our tag. I was given a sleeveless puffa jacket carrying the gang's logo of a skull and crossbones. Brother Chris gave me the bell off his handlebars which looked like a birdcage. Brother Roda Dua gave me a set of waterproof overalls because I didn't have any, and Brother Aal his helmet bag. In return I presented them with Doris's number plate, which I'd been carrying as a memento ever since I abandoned her in Caboolture. It was the most treasured item I carried and I wanted them to have it as a mark of my appreciation.

Before leaving, I sat outside with Brother Roda Dua on a couple of stools, sharing stories about our two countries and doing our best to compare them. He told me about crime in his country and how they hardly have any. He said if a burglar is caught, he will get a beating from the community he stole from. If he, or she, is caught doing it again, then they're in big trouble, sometimes being beaten to death. Same goes for anyone who kills. The police often decide not to get involved and let the community deal with the person as they see fit. As you can imagine, that doesn't end too well for the criminal.

Ignoring the danger of knee-jerk vigilante killing for a minute, I have to say, it did seem wholly effective. People here rarely stole from one another. And I felt very safe. Crime was minimal, all because there was a fear of the consequences. Compare that to our societies. There certainly seemed to be a real sense of responsibility and consequence here, and so it was sad to hear Roda Dua express his desire for his country to be more like ours.

In many ways I couldn't blame him. He'd see our iPods and air tickets taking us to all these places, and you couldn't blame him for thinking, 'Life in England sure must be wonderful.' He'd ask about our health system and I'd say, 'Yes, it's free', and about our welfare system and I'd say, 'Yes, it pays people not to work', which to anyone in their right mind sounds brilliant. We talked about the gear I was carrying — the laptop, the helmet camera, the SLR — and he asked how much I'd paid. You could read it in his face that he assumed I was rich, and I guess I was, compared to him. I tried explaining that as a percentage of our wages it's not so much. Which of course made him think we all get paid like millionaires in the West.

To try and convince him that his world wasn't so bad, I told him about the level of crime in our country, not to mention the massive problem of homelessness in places like Sydney and London, which he just didn't believe. I explained that to afford these iPods and flight tickets we have to work tirelessly in offices, factories and cafés, and that if we ever lost those jobs and couldn't swiftly find another we would no longer be able to afford to pay the massive mortgages and debts most of us have, leaving us in big trouble because unlike their solid families, ours are fragmented. Neither are we self-sufficient nor are our societies geared up to allow people to survive on pennies. I explained that, unlike Indonesians, we rarely smiled, which comes from knowing we are locked in a constant cycle of competition with one another — because that's just how our world works.

But I could tell that he didn't want to believe any of that. He saw England and the Western world in general as models that his country should aspire to. That was his dream for Indonesia. And by the sounds of things, the transformation had already begun. Credit cards, he told me, were being embraced by those living in the cities. The banks were giving them out casually and as a result people were getting into the sorts of financial trouble anyone would if one day they were given a magic piece of plastic allowing them to buy all the things they'd previously been unable to afford. Paying for much of this trip by MasterCard and Visa I was in no position to criticise. It just seemed tragic that their aspirations to become a 'better' country were leading them up a path that might not lead to a place as good as they imagined.

I wished he could have seen, as I saw, the ways in which we could learn things from his country. I loved that a real sense of community spirit prevailed, that people did still eat together and watch out for one another. And that they did still smile and welcome strangers like me into their homes without fear or judgement. I loved how beautifully simple their lives were, how they worked for themselves, how they were self-sufficient, how they dealt with criminals. And yet, having said all that, I still wouldn't trade places and move to Indonesia, and that, maybe, was his point after all.

From there it was back to the road, riding non-stop, flat-out, to make the port town of Belawan at the northern tip of Sumatra before the visa ran out. The roads, as I said, were terrible, non-existent in places. I even had some problems with camping. For a second night I slept wild, beneath another abandoned shelter — this one on stilts — down a steep slope a stone's throw from the road. I had no problem riding Dot down the slope but it rained in the night and the next morning the ground was too muddy to get her back up. It was 6 a.m., jungle all around, and as many times as I tried she got halfway and then either ran out of power or grip, or both.

Finally I gave up trying, dumped all my gear at the bottom of the slope, then dragged her to the top, inch by inch. I was knackered and covered in sweat and mud by the time we made it. I repacked all my gear and put on my helmet, but I just couldn't get Dot to fire into life. Clearly she was flooded from all the time she'd spent on her side. I changed the plug but that didn't work, neither did swearing. Then from nowhere a local man on a scooter appeared. He stopped and tried to help but he couldn't get her going either. He motioned me to climb onboard and for what seemed like a mile this poor man in sandals pushed me and Dot as hard as he could, until finally Dot cleared her lungs and burst into life. The man got back on his bike and rode off. And that's my fondest memory of Sumatra.

8

Malacca

Leaving Indonesia

The ferry from Belawan in Sumatra to Penang in Malaysia wouldn't take motorbikes, only foot passengers. It wouldn't have been so bad but I only discovered this after a man with many promises had told me otherwise and I'd spent a good hour stripping Dot of all her panniers and draining her tanks of fuel in preparation for the ferry's arrival. I gave the drained fuel to the crowd of men looking on, and became increasingly excited at the thought of finally leaving Indonesia behind. It had only been four weeks since we left East Timor, but it felt like a lifetime. Now I just wanted to move on to Malaysia. But when the ferry captain came ashore, he took one look at Dot and said, 'No motorcycles.' I could see it myself; there was no way of getting her onboard.

There were no cargo boats either, none that anyone knew of anyway. That left me standing at the docks, looking out across the water, no way of getting Dot across, and no way was I leaving her behind. The vultures laughed as I bolted the panniers back on and wheeled Dot outside. 'No besin,' they said, pointing at my empty tank and laughing some more because from here back to town I would have to push. I turned the fuel cock to reserve, petrol gushing from the standard tank hidden beneath the seat and into the carburettors below. They hadn't realised I'd got two tanks and that I'd only drained one because I'm not as daft as I look. When Dot fired into life I laughed back at them and rode off.

Heading into town, the weight of the situation really started to worry me. My Indonesian visa expired in the morning and I had no way of getting Dot off the island. That felt pretty dire. To make matters worse the port town of Belawan was a sinister place, not one I wished to linger in. I parked Dot in the shadows and walked along the main street. It was mid-afternoon, still very hot, still very dusty and with so many motorbikes still swarming about. Men with pedal taxis lounging in the shadows called out, 'Hey mister, where do you go, where you from?' I wanted to be rude to them and tell them to leave me alone; instead I smiled and pointed up the road towards the internet café I'd seen on my way through. I hoped I might find some answers online.

Searching through the pages of Horizons Unlimited, a website populated and read by people riding across the world on motorbikes (because I'm not the only one), I found reference to a local man named Mr Monte. Someone travelling this way in the past said he'd hired him to take his motorcycle across the Strait in some kind of vegetable boat. This was as good a lead as I'd got. I paid the owner of the interent place, a friendly woman with a gorgeous daughter who said she would make me a great wife, and rode back to the docks determined to find this mysterious man, attempting to muster some courage and determination as I went. I had a trick for doing this. I would brace my arms against the handlebars, tense, then scream at myself, 'COME ON!' over and over again. 'COME ON!' I barged back into the nest of vultures who I'd given my petrol to earlier, asking, nay, demanding, to know if they'd heard of this Mr Monte.

I was met by a wall of blank expressions. It was as though this man had never even existed, which left me feeling more desolate than before. Literally, I was about to sink to my knees, when someone took pity on me, suggesting that I go and see the harbourmaster, who I found on the top floor of a nearby building, his office overlooking the Strait of Malacca. It was this stretch of water I was desperate to cross. I did my best to explain this to the harbourmaster, a white-haired, weathered old man in a smart uniform, repeating the word 'Honda', moving my hand like a fish, and then pointing towards Malaysia. He poured me a glass of tea as he listened, pondering my problem which he now understood. In broken English, he suggested he might just be able to help.

Down we went to another office. He introduced me to three men: one young, one old, one fat. They were pleasant and told me to have a nap on the bench while they talked amongst themselves. The harbourmaster came and went. It was as though the cogs of an almighty wheel were slowly beginning to turn. Something was being sorted out. I just sat there, listening, wondering what would happen next. The door burst open and through it pushed Forest Whitaker from *The Last King of Scotland* — at least that's who he looked like. You could sense he was the boss immediately, stout and full of menace. He shook my hand. I did my fish to Malaysia gesture again and he demanded I follow him outside to where his moped was parked alongside Dot. 'Follow me,' he said.

We set off on our bikes on a race across the docks, darting between warehouses, turning left and right, two motorbikes in hot pursuit of one another, splashing through puddles and ramming piles of cardboard boxes. This being a Saturday there was no one else around, no vehicles, no people, nothing in this huge sprawling dockland other than me, riding Dot, following a moped ridden by the Last King of Scotland, the sun still baking hot. Finally he turned up a ramp and onto a platform, disappearing through an open door that led into a huge empty warehouse in which we stopped, right in the middle, and got off our bikes. We climbed a set of stairs into an office overlooking the warehouse floor. He turned and stared me straight in the eye. 'I take motorcycle to Malaysia for one million rupiah,' he said. That was almost sixty quid, $120. Out here that was a lot of money. But he must have sensed my desperation and priced accordingly.

Had I trusted my gut I would have walked right out of there; I didn't have a good feeling about any of it.

'When?' I asked.

'You leave motorcycle here and it go Penang in three day.'

He said I should get the passenger ferry that sailed the same day as the bike. I had no choice but to accept his offer. I nodded my head and gave him the cash. I asked for a receipt. 'Not necessary,' he said, and that was that. I took all my electrical gear and a change of clothes from Dot's panniers and stuffed them into a rucksack and left everything else I owned in Dot's locked aluminium box. I gave her one last glance back as we rode away, me on the back of Forest Whitaker's bike; he dropped me back in town. There was nowhere for me to stay in Belawan, so I caught a minibus to Medan, the nearest city, an hour away. In the three days I spent there, I managed to be tricked into buying dinner for a group of local students who befriended me. They handed me the bill and then they ran off.

Finally, I caught the four-hour ferry to Malaysia — overstaying my visa by three days — hoping Dot would be waiting for me at the other end. It was a nervous ride. I expected the worst. But sure enough, when we landed in Panang, there she was, my postie bike from Caboolture. Just one problem: she was being held hostage and to get her back I would have to pay the same fee again to the agent on this side of the Strait of Malacca, a word, coincidently, which in Greek means wanker. I paid this Mr Lim another one million rupiah and I was allowed to ride Dot away from the docks. He said I shouldn't have paid anything at the Indonesian end. That left me a little bitter. But never mind. Me and Dot, somehow, had just ridden 6000 kilometres across the terrible roads of Indonesia in three weeks, catching ferries, hitting buses, falling off several times, eating intestine. And now we were in Malaysia. Good progress.

9

Tea Break

Malaysia

Arriving in Malaysia was the moment when the wheels could finally come to a stop. There was nowhere for me to be, no visa to rush for, no urgency to be anywhere. And for two months and 11,000 kilometres I'd not experienced that before. There'd always been something — whether it was getting up and riding every day, or waiting for Dot's boat to arrive, or even just coping with the unease I'd felt in East Timor — there'd always been something to do or focus on, and now there was nothing. This fourth country sprawled out in front of me and I could go off in any direction I wanted, at whatever pace I wished.

And that was strangely daunting. Because I had options, and by now I realised that with options come decisions and with decisions comes indecision. I wasn't exactly sure what I was going to do. I could ride down to Kuala Lumpur, or even carry on to Singapore. I could visit the tropical islands off the northern coastline. Or I could turn left and skip Malaysia completely and ride straight into Thailand and carry on with the journey. Admittedly, having to choose between those options wasn't such a bad position to be in, but it did make me wish for another deadline and another place we *had* to be because then the decision would have been made for me.

While I tried to make up my mind I spent a few days doing laundry in Penang, an island just off the mainland with beach resorts popular with package holiday-makers. There is also a main town which was just a nice place to be. At night there was an eerie glow from the street lighting and the small clusters of food stalls and markets around which everyone gathered. The craftsmen and store owners worked well into the night in their tiny little lairs, which you could peep into as you passed, a single bulb illuminating their stitching, or fabricating, or book-keeping. It was a productive town, also with backpackers about, the most I'd seen in one place since Darwin.

I didn't feel like a backpacker, though; I felt like someone who'd just crawled out of a hedge-bottom, or out from the bleak black wood and was now stumbling to my feet with twigs in my hair and covered in the leaves of an autumn chill. Watching the new arrivals shuffle nervously about in the street made me realise just how much I'd acclimatised and adapted to my surroundings. After all, I'd been like that myself, probably worse, back in East Timor, cowering with my head in my hands at the airport the day I arrived. Now I walked with a weary knowledge of the world and an acceptance of its nature to scare and to thrill. Though I don't think I was scared any more, or worried; I knew by now that things always have a way of working themselves out, and if you just keep riding, you'll get there.

It was a nice feeling. I felt like I could just stand with my two feet on the spot and survey the world around me rather than cower from it as I'd previously done. It had been a steep learning curve coming through Indonesia and, while at times I hated the place and the hurdles it posed for me, now I was grateful for the test it had set. It had made me stronger and educated me in the rules of travel, and survival and fending for myself. Most of all it had taught me to live with uncertainty and no longer to fear it or worry about the things you can't have a hand in shaping. I think in a way that's the only skill, if you want to call it that, that you need for a journey like this — just a willingness to live an uncertain existence. Not knowing where you're going to stay or where you're going to arrive that night.

I suppose with the way I set off at such short notice I didn't have much choice but to learn to live with uncertainty, and that was all right; it gets quite exciting after a while, not knowing where you're going to be the next night or how you're going to get there. It keeps you on your toes and always guessing and wondering, and without a plan or a blueprint I didn't have to worry that I wasn't sticking to it, or getting to the wrong place at the wrong time. I could be anywhere and still be in the right place. All I had to do was ride along, trying to make as much progress as I could every day and be happy with that. And it didn't seem to matter that I wasn't very good on a bike or a good navigator, or sharp minded, or anything else. I was a fool, muddling through and quite enjoying the way Dorothy and my riding gear drew empathy from the locals, maybe sometimes ridicule, but never resentment. At least none that I detected.

Had this been me in isolation, things might have been plain sailing. But it wasn't just me, it was me and Mandy, still trying to maintain something, trying to keep the pair of us together throughout all this, or at least not come to the point of silence. And there is no doubt that it is the person who is left behind who suffers most in a situation like this. They are the ones with the routine and the time to sit on the porch drinking their wine just wondering if a motorbike is going to come around that corner having decided to turn back. They are the ones who feel the distance growing bigger, who feel the silence of the empty inbox that goes on for days and days, who wonder why you haven't called, who wonder where you are, and what you're doing as you're camped out in the Indonesian wild.

Imagine yourself in their position and ask yourself just how long do you wait, how long do you give someone to live their dream and possibly come back again? Forever? Or do you move on and leave them to it as it must at times be so tempting to do? I know Mandy had been the one who gave me the push to do this, but it had been my idea, one which I'd continued to talk about and told her I'd really like to do one day, even perhaps to the detriment of me finding a way to stay. How do you reconcile that? 'He tells me he loves me and wants to be with me but he wants to ride across the world on a motorbike.' You can imagine what must have gone through her mind after the dust had settled and I'd ridden out of town: 'That's all right, but what do I get out of this?'

A holiday at least, because in a month's time Mandy would be meeting me in Thailand, landing in Bangkok and staying for two weeks. We'd been talking about it all the way from Timor, trying to figure out some dates and work out if it would be good for us or not. Of course it would. It hadn't been an easy time between here and Sydney, for either of us. In fact, without doubt, this was the greatest challenge of them all, making this work, trying to keep it together. It made riding a motorbike across the world seem very easy in comparison, even getting a boat from the Belawan dock. Now I was just really looking forward to showing her my world. And sharing it.

My main problem in the meantime would be money. By now my mum had emailed in great panic over the state of my finances after she'd been brave enough to open one of my bank statements. In her words it was time to come home. That was perhaps her general worry as much as anything else, and I knew I couldn't do that, not now, not having come this far and having placed so much importance on the completion of this thing. It was the purchase of Dot and the Carnet, not to mention the couple of grand I was still owed, that had tipped me into the red. All I could do was extend my overdraft and make a call to the bank to up the limit on a credit card. I also had a great friend from university, a guy called Paul Taylor, who right from the start had offered to lend me some cash if I ever fell short. I emailed him from Malaysia and asked if I could borrow a bit to tide me over until the money came through. Self-sufficiency went out the window; I now had a back-up crew.

Though in a way I always had; I'd just never realised it. At the beginning, as I crossed the Harbour Bridge, I claimed that my destiny was in my own two hands, but over time I'd accepted that it wasn't, not entirely anyway. Instead, it was in the hands of the many people who had already helped me along the way. The men who had fixed the road in Australia, the captains of the ferries who took me from one Indonesian island to another, the man who drove me to Darwin airport at 5 a.m. to catch my plane. They are the cogs that make all this happen, they are the people who don't travel and allow others to do so. Now I had Paul to thank, a friend who'd worked solidly ever since leaving university to put some money together so that he was able to lend a hand when one of his friends set off across the world on a motorbike without enough money. And for that I shall be forever grateful. Just as I was to the mechanic I found in Penang who gave Dot a tune-up for free.

It was the baker next door to the guesthouse who had directed me to him, drawing me a map and warning me that this man was very selective about the bikes he fixed. Navigating the town's back alleys, I pulled up outside his workshop, stacked floor to ceiling with motorcycle parts. The mechanic, a white-haired man in his sixties, took one look at Dot and was immediately smitten. He'd never seen such a thing. 'From Australia?' he gasped, recognising the engine and some of the other components fitted to the bikes he fixed in Malaysia. Of course he would work on her, and in no time at all he'd set the valve clearance and cleaned the carburettor and sent me down the road for a test ride. She felt brand new again, the postie bike that had just brought me 11,000 kilometres from Caboolture.

Dot's story is interesting. She began life as a mail delivery machine around the suburbs of Queensland. At 30,000 kilometres she was retired, and like all postie bikes, sold at auction. Hers took place in Brisbane, where she was bought by Joe of One Ten Motorcycles to sell in his shop in Caboolture. One day, a little later, a man named Colin walked through the shop door. Colin, fifty-six, had just spent two years sailing his yacht around the Queensland coast. He was now after a new challenge, one on land, his search somehow leading him to Joe's shop, where from a line-up of identical machines he picked one. With big ambitions for this bike, Colin fitted bright orange panniers, a lamb's-wool seat, a handlebar brace, a long-range fuel tank, and even heavy duty inner tubes and tyres. Now the pair were ready to tackle the great Australian Outback.

They started with a two-week trip west to Canarvon Gorge, where his new machine was faultless. Their second outing was even longer, a four-week ride up to Birdsville and then on to the Flinders Ranges, Broken Hill, along the Darling River and on to Bourke and Brisbane — a 4500-kilometre trip on which the only thing that went wrong was two bolts falling out of the mudguard mount. Colin developed quite a bond with his bike — he used to talk to her — and it was with real sadness that he parted with it, selling the little red machine back to Joe. That was the end of 2008. A little over a month later I rushed into the same shop in desperate need of help in getting to England. The name Colin gave his bike: Dorothy.

Now that same machine was propelling me out of Penang, across the massive bridge and onto the mainland, the pair of us heading for a region of Malaysia called the Cameron Highlands. It wasn't far away, but it was a steep climb, the road twisting higher and higher into the cloudy sky and past endless fields of tea — this is where the country's plantations are. The air was cool and crisp, refreshing after so long at sea level. They also grow strawberries here, and the greenhouses are a popular stop with tourist buses, which stay just long enough to allow the passengers to pick their own. Me and Dorothy passed them on our climb to the town of Tanah Rata, a small place nestled right at the heart of it, surrounded by trees and with walks to little waterfalls and a main street packed with restaurants and even a Starbucks.

It must have been good coffee, as the price of a cup was the same as I was paying for a night in the hostel. The hostel was up a lane with decrepit houses either side, its front wall covered in graffiti. Outside were sofas on which travellers from all over the world sat, even some from Iran, who gave me their addresses and told me to give them a call on the way through as they would show me around. (I wasn't really going through Iran, was I?) The hostel's best feature was its camp fire every evening, around which everyone gathered, telling stories, drinking flavoured tea, and, if feeling extravagant, cooking bananas and chocolate in tinfoil over the flames. There might be a dozen of us, sitting up late, or retiring early, maybe to watch a film in the TV lounge. *Into the Wild* was a popular choice. Then we'd all go to bed in our two-dollar dorms.

I only planned on staying a night, but ended up there a week. They were a good bunch, and at times like these I realised just how much I enjoyed meeting people on the road. It's almost as though the awkwardness of the introductory process is completely removed, because you might only have that one conversation and never see each other again, allowing you to be totally frank and honest with each other — no searching for thoughts or what you think is the right word; you just say what's on the tip of your tongue. And you seem to find out so much more about each other that way. Equally, if you want to sit in silence in the corner and get drunk on the vapours of your mind, then you could do that as well.

Finally, after a week in the Cameron Highlands, I woke one morning to find everyone in the hostel had vanished. All the people I'd been hanging out with had suddenly disappeared, whisked away on the tourist conveyer belt that looped around the country. That left the hostel very quiet and empty, a shell of the place it had been before. I didn't like the feeling and made a mental note to make sure that I was never the last person to leave a place. There's no one to wave you goodbye; you just have to pack up in silence, carry your gear to the bike and buckle up.

As I loaded Dorothy with all my gear I thought about going on a mad dash around Laos, Cambodia and Vietnam, but deep down I didn't have the heart or the energy for it; I didn't have the money either. And in all seriousness, I didn't think it wise to go off gallivanting down side roads when Dot still had 20,000 kilometres or more left to go. I certainly didn't want her collapsing a distance from the border equal to the length of the detour I made just so I could check out a temple, or even look around Singapore. My gut was telling me to move the trip forward, get to the next country where in a few weeks' time the girl I'd missed so much would be landing. With that decision made, I kicked Dot into life and headed for the border.

10

Night Rider

Malaysia–Thailand Border

The mountain road was much faster on the way down, tea fields flashing by either side, and even on the skinny tyres bought in Indonesia for five dollars Dot handled the corners with confidence, rolling from left to right and happy to lean as far as I dared push her. Which wasn't very far to be fair, but it was just a nice place to be riding, dipping down through the clouds and staring out to the green Malaysian carpet below. The temperature warmed the closer we got to sea level, and off came the clothes, back to the shorts and striped English shirt rolled up to the elbow. I should really be grateful that I never fell off dressed like this as I would have been skinned alive.

The intention was to cross the border that afternoon and cover a couple of hundred kilometres on the other side before nightfall. It was wishful thinking, because not long after joining the slick highway I felt the rear end skew about and the steel wheel make direct contact with the ground. I ducked off the highway and down the slip road of a motorway service station and pulled up. Ahead of me was a petrol station. Above was the shade of a tree, to my left a line of food stalls and some seats where people sat watching as I jumped off in frustration, turning the air blue with my cursing before lifting up the back end of my motorcycle on a brick and getting out my tools.

A couple of road sweepers stood smoking cigarettes a metre away from where my sweat hit the ground. I'd had enough punctures by now to know the procedure, but I still found the whole process an ordeal. Take off the axle bolt and two rear brake calliper nuts, knock out the axle with a hammer, flop Dot on her side to allow her wheel to fall out and hey presto, there you have it, a tyre free to repair. A passing group of smartly dressed men stopped to help, and in no time at all we stood like proud parents as Dot rested on her new back wheel. We took photos, and shook oily hands; as they left, I looked back — the tyre had gone flat again. Then it started raining.

Now on my own, I put Dot on the brick, took out the wheel, levered off the tyre and found a nail I'd not removed the first time round. With no more new inner tubes I mended the old one at the service station. An elderly Chinese man held a brolly over my head while I stuck a plaster over the blowing hole. He didn't say much, nor did I. A nod of despair was all that was needed. We smiled, looked up at the heavens, and shook our heads, the rain now falling heavier than ever. The wheel went back on, the tools were put away and this time, finally, Dot's wheel didn't go flat. Back to the road.

I'd never seen it rain so hard, not even in the Outback

during the 'wet'. Every time a lorry passed by it caused a bow wave that would come rolling towards us with such force that I would be sodden and Dot would judder to suggest she wasn't coping too well. I threatened to pull off the road a couple of times and find a place to put the tent up, but there were too many people and houses about. Gone were the little lanes to views over rolling hills; the world around us was flat and mostly agricultural, with patches of industry. At least the water was warm and the waterproof jacket and trousers the BigZoners had set me up with were doing a decent job of keeping the rain out. Even if my basketball boots and mismatched gloves were not. I now wore one beige, one black studded leather glove. Thankfully I'd lost opposing hands so could still make a pair.

Two hours later, dripping wet, I made it to the border. It was 9 p.m., almost fully dark and still spitting with rain. As Thailand doesn't recognise the Carnet de Passage, foreigners travelling to the country with their own vehicle are instead issued with a temporary import slip covering them for thirty days. At the bottom of this form, in small print, just below the signature, it reads that if you aren't out of the country within that period, you'd be issued with a fine of 420,000 Thai baht. That's the equivalent of 15,000 Australian dollars, which seems rather steep, and given that I would need to be in the country a little longer than thirty days, I was relieved to hear you can have it extended at any of the borders around the country.

As for a place to stay that night, the border guard advised me to sleep in Hat Yai, the first major town I'd come to, perhaps an hour or so away. This was going to be interesting because the city, and in fact the whole southern region of Thailand, has a travel warning against it — meaning no insurance — due to the sporadic fighting that takes place there. It's a secret war, waged by Muslims in the region who claim to have had land taken from them by the Thai government. Almost a hundred civilians had been killed in bomb blasts over the past few years, with several detonating in Hat Yai alone. Given the 'trouble' in East Timor, I wasn't too fazed by this. I was sure I'd be fine.

The road leading to the city was an interesting one. It was lined with sex bars, lit up with neon, all with girls standing outside in their underwear trying to lure the truckers who would be passing through this route. Apparently the scene is also popular with Malaysians heading over the border on 'business trips'. I didn't see many people this night. The road was eerily quiet. I stopped at a cash machine for some local currency and there was no one else about. The weather, though, was now warm and my clothes completely dry. I was excited about being in Thailand, especially with Mandy arriving in just a few weeks' time.

Past midnight I found the only hostel in Hat Yai. It was up a flight of stairs with an unfriendly man on reception who reluctantly showed me one of the rooms. It was off a dark, creepy corridor, much like those in an American high school horror movie, and while I'd slept in far worse places I just didn't want to sleep there that night. 'No thank you,' I said to the man as I walked back down the stairs and through the door into the empty moonlit street. No traffic about, just me,

Dot and silence. If I were a smoker, I would have lit one now, taking a drag as some cool blues music played inside my head. An old newspaper would have tumbled across the street, a distant dog would have barked, steam would have risen from a vent in the wet empty black road. I didn't need to sleep, I needed to ride, through the night. 'Phuket Dot, that's where we'll head.'

I rode back through the town and out along one of the main streets, stopping at a local convenience store, which must surely have been the only one for miles around owned by a middle-aged Yorkshireman. He had a Thai wife and had lived there for many years. I couldn't quite believe it; it just seemed so random. It was late at night in Thailand, in a city deep in the country's south, and I was in a convenience store owned by a man who once lived in the same county as my parents, who was able to draw me a map of the area because I didn't have one, and who served me coffee and engaged me in interesting conversation. Weighing up all that, I deemed him one of Denise's fairies and quite possibly a figment of my imagination because he couldn't possible have been real. I carried on my way, the fairy's map strapped to my petrol tank for guidance.

Out on the open road, well shot of the city, I squinted to see in Dot's dim headlight, following the main road that would take us through Phatthalung, Trang and Huai Yot, on our way to Phuket. I guessed it to be a distance of 400 kilometres, the plan to get there in time for breakfast. Though at a time like this, if the tank didn't run dry or if I didn't get hungry or need to take a pee, I think I could have ridden forever and ever, because it was just such a great sensation — that feeling of getting somewhere, of covering ground, especially at night with no one else on the road. It felt like you've got the whole world to yourself, like you were seeing the things all the others were missing while they were tucked up in bed. There's a golden rule of adventure motorcycling that says not to ride at night because of the danger. But what about the beauty and the magic that come alive at the witching hour? I'll accept any risk for a little taste of that.

The only problem, of course, is sleep. By 2 a.m. I could feel myself drifting off, my chin hitting my chest until I snapped back to life and returned to the centre of the road. Eventually, I had to accept the danger in this and began looking for a decent spot by the side of the road to pitch the tent, but it was too dark to find one. The best I could do was a bus shelter in the middle of nowhere, so I rode Dot into it, lay the wicker mat from the Timor ferry I shared with the spitting bitch on the seat, and took a nap. I set my alarm clock to go off in forty-five minutes, but it seemed to ring only a split-second later, waking me up in the darkness on a bench in a bus stop with the knife in my hand, just in case. I got up and hit the road, now around 3 a.m.; still no one else around.

By 5 a.m. I was tired again, so I snoozed on another bench, waking with the sun as my alarm clock. This time when I hit the road the people of southern Thailand were starting to stretch and yawn. Perhaps it wasn't as beguiling as the Australian Outback at a similar time of day, but it was still beautiful, and seemingly more interesting than Malaysia, even if I was still a long way from Phuket. My plan to make it there in time for breakfast had been scuppered by punctures and sleeping, and to ride on in this tired state would have been suicide. Instead I settled for a town called Krabi, pulling into its waterfront streets after almost twenty-four hours on the road. I was absolutely knackered and looked disgusting. Worse still, in that moment I realised I'd forgotten to buy the mandatory third-party insurance back at the border, now the distance between Sydney and Canberra away. It meant the next day I had no choice but to ride back and get it.

11

Making Friends and Influencing Embassies

Thailand

Krabi was in a beautiful spot, right where the Krabi River joined the Andaman Sea. *The Beach* and *The Man with the Golden Gun* were filmed just a short boat ride away. Even if I hadn't known that, I still might have guessed it given those familiar-looking towering blocks of stone that grew from the earth and from the ocean floor. At times, when they were lit in silhouette, the cliffs and rock stacks gave the impression of a city skyline. Were it not for these structures the world around would have been completely flat. There were no hills or even any tall trees, just clusters of jungle sitting below a sky of vivid blue.

The hostel I stayed in was on the road along the waterfront. It was only a small place, in the same row of buildings as the travellers' bookshops and cafés and other guesthouse-restaurants. The wooden-walled room cost a couple of dollars a night.

There were no windows, only a single bare light bulb swinging above a spring bed. It was a shed. But I hardly spent any time in there, preferring to go for a stroll around the bustling market in the centre of town or walk along the waterfront saying 'No thank you' to the men trying to get me to book a boat ride. Of an evening, the owner of the guesthouse — a large, scary-looking woman who one day knocked Dot over and was nice to us after that — would allow me to wheel Dot inside the small restaurant, clearing the tables and chairs to make room, so she would be safe at night.

Keith was staying at the guesthouse too. In his fifties, he was ex-military, and told some incredible stories about his army days and more recently those he'd spent on the road. I asked him if he ever considered moving home to England and settling down, to which he said he didn't have a home. I felt sorry for him; I guess everyone needs a home, even if sometimes we're not always entirely sure where it is (where you were born, where you feel you belong, where your heart is?). Keith spent his time going backwards and forwards between India, Nepal and Indonesia, travelling, living off his pension, telling stories to strangers like me and Will, an eighteen-year-old English lad who wasn't sure if he was enjoying his first experience of backpacking or not. He'd considered going home early, which I think is a natural urge on your first time away from home. I know I'd been the same when I'd done a skiing season in France at the age of eighteen. The sense that with so much at home, why would you possibly want to be here?

INDIA
CHINA
EXPENSIVE GUIDE REQUIRED
MYANMAR (BURMA)
BORDERS CLOSED
LAOS
CHIANG MAI
THAILAND
BANGKOK
TOTAL TIME: 2 MONTHS
DISTANCE COVERED NOT SURE
CAMBODIA
COULDN'T BRING MYSELF TO TRAVEL EAST
KO CHANG
VIETNAM
PHUKET
KRABI
HAT YAI
PENANG
CAMERON HIGHLAND
MALAYSIA
FREE VISA/3 MONTHS
MEDAN
INDONESIA
SINGAPORE

It was a tough time then for Will. I felt for him; perhaps he came for answers, and like the rest of us only found more questions. And so to cheer him up, the pair of us went off on a boat cruise, five islands in a day, offering us the opportunity to masquerade as proper tourists: snorkelling, eating packed lunches, that sort of thing. The boat was especially cool — narrow and wooden, with seats facing each other and a flapping canopy overhead. The captain stood at the back, operating what looked to be an old diesel engine from a lorry with a propeller mounted on a long drive shaft. It was noisy and smelly and quite in contrast to the stunning water world we were cruising through, those pillars of rock casting shadows all around. I'm not sure if any of us found our 'beach' that day, but we sure did look. Whether we were looking in the right place, though, I'm not so certain. Something tells me it's not made of sand.

The next day I reunited with Dot and rode out to the nearby Tiger Temple. I'd been told that if you had the patience, and the sweat, to climb exactly 1237 steps, then you would be rewarded with the same vantage point as the three-storey high statue of Buddha that had been built at the summit. I climbed, taking an age and having to use my hands to haul myself up as monkeys slid down the handrail like kids down a banister. The steps were steep, chiselled roughly into the rock and giving way to sheer drops. After an hour or so I made it, podgy, unfit, beetroot red, shadow boxing at the top of those Philadelphia steps like Rocky.

I stood and looked out at the sea and the land now so very far below. Such a great view from up there, the place so calm and peaceful, no one else about but a groundkeeper sweeping the dust from the tiled floor that surrounded Buddha's feet. The summit of this pillar of stone was a great place to stand and think, first about jumping off (in the weird way that high places always make you do), and then about what it must have taken to have built such a thing. I suspect it starts with people brave enough to climb it, strong enough to carry the rock to the top of it and skilled enough to build on it. Then you need people persistent enough to finish it, devoted enough to climb it for daily prayer, and also tolerant enough to let people of different faiths visit it for free.

I watched a plane flying overhead. Maybe it was the altitude making me mental, but I stood there thinking, 'We did that … humans.' Conceived, designed and built a flying metal tube that shuts the door on one world, hurtles down a runway, takes off, defies gravity, serves you a meal, shows you a movie, brings you beer and some nuts, then nine hours later or whatever it is, lands without exploding in a totally different part of the world where everything you know has been turned on its head. The same device then scoops up a load of people wanting to go the other way and gives them the same sensation, only in reverse. Riding that sort of distance on a motorbike sure does make you appreciate how cool that is.

A few days later, I found myself in Bangkok just in time to see the political protests kick off. This was June 2009. A news bulletin told me the number of policemen killed, bullets fired, vehicles set ablaze. Kevin Rudd, the man who had signed my helmet in the Glebe bookshop, had cancelled his trip to the city and advised everyone else to do the same. He said it wasn't safe, which I considered an overreaction, given that I and three German backpackers were able to sit and drink a Chang beer in the hostel bar, just a short walk from where hundreds of thousands of the protestors had gathered in red T-shirts. I never fully understood the dispute, knowing only that it was about a Prime Minister some people didn't like, but clearly it was important to a great deal of them. Though was this really the same city as they were showing on the news? The same one that Mr Rudd advised us not to go to? It was.

It was fascinating to see for myself just how much the media twist things, but if anything, that gave me hope for the road ahead. Pakistan was now looming ever closer on the horizon. Every time I turned on the television another bomb had gone off and more people had fallen to the turmoil there. The newsreaders told me the Taliban were surging, that their 'army' might take over Islamabad within a few weeks. To think I was intending to ride through there on a postie bike was a little harrowing, but I had great hope that the reality would be the same as the one I'd experienced in Bangkok. That I would get there and find that the media had exaggerated the situation and that people there were no different to people anywhere else I'd met on my travels, and, that if I kept my head down, I would have no trouble at all quietly passing through. Beyond Nepal, beyond India, I guess I would find out for myself.

For now, though, I was really growing to like Bangkok. I might again sound naive, but I expected it to be an ugly, polluted city, made up of shanty towns and quite primitive, flooded with women on their backs firing ping pong balls for men to catch. But it wasn't like that at all. The main centre was full of huge glass-towered shopping malls with names of all the Western stores that we might know. I saw expensive German cars and even a Lamborghini. Not being an economist I couldn't quite figure how with such a weak currency they could afford to build and buy such things given some of it would have to be imported. The traffic fines surely must have helped — the police stopped and fined me and Dot twice, for various things, but mainly because we were riding like a pair of maniacs.

The city's backpacker scene was largely confined to just one road, Khao San, closed off to traffic but open to all manner of pedlars flogging things that are cheap but which you'll never need. You had to be careful walking along it. Sellers would ask if you wanted to buy something or go in a bar and you'd say, 'No, next time', and carry on walking. When you walked back later that day they would have remembered your face and say, 'So you come in now?' and you'd have to make some other excuse. Men at each end of the road would try and lure you into a tuk-tuk, then on the way to your destination, they would spend three hours insisting you go into tailors and jewellery stores so that they'd get their fuel vouchers. Con artists and tricksters, found everywhere tourists go.

That's why I stayed in a guesthouse a twenty-minute walk away from Khao San, in an area called Thewet, along the river, out where families — and the rioters — lived. It was a great place to see typical Thai life. The guesthouse fronted on to a square with a market in the middle and houses and shops around the edge. Next door was a tiny alcohol merchant's with men sitting outside on wooden crates playing draughts and chequers and sinking beers, while across the road an old woman with a hunched back lived amongst the garbage she collected and recycled for money. Funnelling off in every direction were rows of food stalls, smelling great, selling everything from meatballs and chicken satay, to chunks of fruit like pineapple and melon that you bought in clear bags and ate with wooden sticks.

At night a van would pull up across the road. A white-haired man, notoriously drunk, would cook up the best noodle soup from a pan mounted on the back of this vehicle. He'd bring it over in a bowl to the blue plastic seat you were sitting on in the middle of the pavement as the sky fell black and the tree-lined street grew largely still. The neon flash of a tuk-tuk would scream past, a pink taxi perhaps, boys on scooters, for sure. I was no longer seeing such places from behind the visor of a speeding helmet; I was now within that world, breathing its fragrant air, eating its food, meeting its people. This was an element of the trip that I'd not anticipated when I'd set off, but I adored it now because I got to see the soul of a city, and not just its sights. I stopped feeling like a traveller, more like a local instead.

What I also liked about Thailand was that it had this beautiful balance between old and new. There were supermarkets like those in Australia and England, convenience stores on every street corner too. Your fuel you could buy from Caltex, your burger from McDonald's, a new camera from the huge electronics department store. You could catch the sky-train, watch an IMAX movie, play arcades, sing in karaoke booths. Yet there were also these back-alley communities where you could eat deep-fried cockroaches from stalls on the street and wander around markets where cats would be licking the meat and buckets of crabs and eels would line up along the floor for you to watch them dying. And then be eaten.

What I also found interesting was the Thais' reverence for their king. His picture hung on all public buildings, on restaurant walls, in people's houses, even in the cinema where you have to stand for a short movie about his life before a film starts. Nobody can criticise him; you can't even stop a rolling coin by putting your foot on it because that would be seen as standing on the king's head. You can't write negative things about him, as a foreign author found out when he got three years' prison for doing just that in his book. I suspect some Thai people loathe this forced worship, though they could never say so in public. But for anyone passing through the country it seems so impressive to observe a whole nation of people tightly aligned around their ruler and also around their religion.

Compare that to, say, England, where neither the queen nor religion means anything to anyone any more. We might see the country unite at the World Cup or when Diana died, but the rest of the time everyone's off laying their cable in different ditches. There seems to be very little that binds us any more. In Thailand you feel a genuine sense of cohesion, people looking out for one another, like the homeless man I saw being given food by the stall holders as he walked through the streets. Or that old woman with the hunched back carving out an existence from the bits of scrap people would give her to sell. And even me, a stranger from a foreign land, passing through on his little red motorbike.

I was on the road one day, somewhere around Bangkok, motoring along, when a teenager pulled alongside on his scooter. He was simply curious as to who I was and where I was heading and we chatted as we rode along the highway, traffic streaming past. Eventually this guy, who's name was Egh, raced off ahead because he was faster than us and we were slowing him down. A short while later he flagged me down. As I stopped he handed me his green and white shell suit jacket, pointing to my arms reddening in the blazing sun, and suggested the jacket would protect me. It was a gift, from a Thai teenager, who, he told me, earned US$200 a month working in a factory, to a Western visitor with a camera worth four times as much. He rode off, leaving me speechless.

Then later, stopping for lunch at a stall on the road between two towns, I got up to pay and the lady serving pointed towards a man getting into a black four-wheel drive. It took a minute to work out what she meant — he had paid my bill — and by that time all I could do was watch him drive away, with no time even to say thanks. I've since read how it's part of Thai culture to give a gift to strangers, which explains things, but still, it makes you feel very humble, and even guilty, for receiving gifts from people who might not have as much as you. But perhaps in other ways they do have more than you, and that's why they can *afford* to give. I liked Thailand a lot. It has a kind soul, and it's full of fairies.

I just wish some of this generosity had rubbed off on the man at the Pakistan Embassy in Bangkok when I went to ask him for a visa.

The first thing he said was, 'You have to apply for a visa in your own country.'

I said, 'That's England.'

'Then that's where you have to go.'

'I can't fly to England just to get a visa and then come back,' I said.

He was adamant; I'd have to. I said there must be another way, and he told me, 'No, go home.' I had no answer to that and was prepared to do so if necessary, calculating the budget implications of a flight home to get a visa, and then to come back again, because I couldn't abandon the trip because of it, when thankfully his colleague told me there might be another way. He explained that if I went to the British Embassy and got them to write a letter confirming they had no objection to me going through Pakistan, then I might just be able to save myself the airfare home, and back again.

Leaving Dot's saddle bags back at the hostel, I was able to race to the embassy through central Bangkok traffic in record time. It was like an arcade game, with me and Dot flat out everywhere we went, squeezing between the gaps in the traffic and racing the brightly coloured taxis and doing anything we could to keep the racing line. I would be dressed in my board shorts and thongs, much like the other scooter boys in the city, and at the traffic lights we would all sit, revving our engines, looking across at each other and up at the towering buildings and the endless concrete jungle. Then the light would turn green and off we'd all shoot, one giant mechanical mass of motorbikes swarming through the city streets.

You could have the best adventure flying into Thailand, picking up a local bike for peanuts and riding it around to your heart's content. You wouldn't need any of the documentation or hassle that I was having on this trip; you could just take off, probably ride into Cambodia and Laos as well, maybe even Vietnam, which is a little trickier to get into with a foreign vehicle, but possible. I'd met a Scottish traveller who'd done just that on a Minsk motorcycle he'd bought here, taking it through the jungle and camping wild, living with the locals and riding endlessly until the bike finally stopped and he abandoned it somewhere, catching a bus back to Bangkok. I was fascinated to hear how easy it was, and cheap. It's clear you could ride in so many directions and camp every step of the way.

I slept in some odd places in Thailand. On those park benches, behind hedges at the side of the road, even on Phuket beach, where I was told to watch out for the prowling lady-boys. Though my favourite of them all was at a national park called Khao Sok. I stopped there on my way from Phuket to Bangkok, discovering a jungle with a little stream and a clearing on which I could pitch my tent. In the afternoon I went for a walk along one of the trails and got covered in leeches, which I scraped off with my knife. I bumped into a German couple with the same problem. We talked for a while as we came back down the trail, and then said goodbye; another set of souls, I thought to myself, I would never meet again.

Back in Bangkok, the British Embassy was an interesting place. As far as I could tell, the room was split into two groups. There was the group of older gentlemen, sitting with younger Thai women who I assume they were hoping to take home as their wives. It looked a strange arrangement, what with them not quite able to communicate, though in a way I could see how that might appeal. The second group were youths who appeared to have lost their passports after getting drunk the night before, and now they were panicking about how they were going to get home. Some of the latter group were real scumbags, swearing at staff, becoming aggressive, just plain rude. I was being judgemental, just as they had every right to be about the hairy son of a bitch in the corner muttering something about a visa for Pakistan.

Finally I was told that the letter would be ready in a week, though in no way, shape or form would the British Government take any responsibility for my trip through Pakistan. I would be on my own, through thick and thin. That realisation was pretty sobering, as in the waiting room I'd watched the BBC News highlight the plight of 500,000 Pakistanis displaced by the fighting. It worried me to see that, but not to the point of having second thoughts; it was more a case of looking at the images and thinking, 'I hope that's all calmed down when *I* get there.' There was almost an inevitability to it now, as though as long as Dot held up then we'd be going to that place on the telly, where the people are being killed. I was resigned to that, almost attracted because I was curious to see it for myself.

The route I planned to follow ran along the southern

corridor of Pakistan, from Lahore to Quetta and then on to the first city in Iran, Bam, which had just been struck by an earthquake. For the last 600 kilometres in Pakistan the road would lead through the bandit land of Balochistan, a dry desert region, well beyond government control and in tribal hands. There, I could expect to be given an armed military escort because the risk of being kidnapped is so high. Armed police even hang around your hotel room overnight, or they may prefer you to sleep in their compound, whichever is safest. The system isn't fool-proof. In the months leading up to this point, a French traveller had been taken from his 4x4 and not seen since, while a Polish contractor had been executed after being abducted from his workplace near Peshawar.

Back at the Pakistan Embassy, the man examined my British Government letter of non-objection and still said no, insisting that it wasn't worded right. I argued with him, making a nuisance of myself. I had to; if I'd walked out of the embassy without a visa that day, I really would have had to fly back to England to get a visa to come back — that's how determined (desperate?) I was to ride a postie bike across the world. Finally he asked, 'What bike are you on anyway?'

'A 105cc Honda post bike,' I said.

He looked up from his paperwork. '500cc?' he asked, not hearing me right.

'No,' I said, 'ONE-HUNDRED-AND-FIVE-cc.'

That made him a laugh. 'That's ridiculous.' I nodded. 'I don't get you people,' he continued. 'Why do you live like this, why don't you go home and get a job?'

I said he sounded like my mother and he laughed again. Then he asked for my passport and A$200 and told me to come back for my visa the following morning. I was getting a ten-day tourist visa for Pakistan, at a notoriously difficult embassy, all because of Dot's tiny engine capacity.

And with that I went to the airport to pick up my visitor.

12

Flying Metal Tube

Thailand

I didn't quite know what to do or say as Mandy walked through the arrivals lounge towards me. Just smile, say, 'Hi, how are you?' and give her the biggest hug, feeling my eyes start to water and my insides turn to mush. I'd missed that hug, and when I closed my eyes I could feel all the turbulence of the past four months just drain away. And what a contrast: me, hairy and scruffy; her, manicured and neat. Beauty and the beast, walking through Bangkok airport, hand in hand. She looked stunning, and I was nervous; I think we were both nervous, because it had been so long. But after a minute, it was just like old times.

I thought it would be a nice surprise to pick her up on Dot — that way she could see what it was like to travel by motorbike. I'd rustled up a spare seat and planned on emptying the contents of her giant rucksack into the panniers and then somehow carrying the rucksack on the bike as the pair of us rode along the main highway, back to the guesthouse, about an hour's ride away. Given the fact that she'd just got off an eleven-hour flight and it was gone 10 p.m., she humoured me really well. But then it became obvious that her gear wasn't going to fit, and it looked like she was about to kill me, so I suggested we get a taxi instead. 'Yes, what a very good idea, Nathan,' she said. Poor old Dot had to stay at the airport overnight.

We sat in the taxi, holding hands. It was pink, the seats were vinyl, I remember that. Mandy was wearing a floral skirt, her hair was in pigtails. I was in combat shorts and wore a tatty black cap I'd bought in Malaysia. We looked out at the city as we approached it, night time, the neon lights burning the darkness away. Skyscrapers drew our vision up, other taxis flew past in the outside lane. We'd been fleeced on ours, paying far too much, but it didn't matter. Tonight it was irrelevant. We smiled. Squeezed hands tighter. So surreal. So brilliant. God, I missed being with her. As good as Dorothy, her surrogate, might have been at conversation on the long lonely roads, it wasn't the same. And so, with Mandy here, I'd found my 'beach'; it was here, in the back of a Bangkok taxi.

The taxi couldn't reach the guesthouse because of the roadblocks, so had to drop us off an hour's walk away. It was midnight, and the only route was right through the centre of the protestors. This was a good opportunity for me to display my heroic composure in the face of confrontation by leading a path through the lot of them. Though really, they couldn't have been nicer, offering us whisky, or at the worst ignoring us, and we stepped over some of them asleep on the pavement, their

Day one, departure. By far the hardest day of them all. If it hadn't been for Immigration – and Mandy – I know I never would have ridden from Sydney to London on a postie bike.

'All the best, K. Rudd, P. Minister.' I asked his security guard before approaching the PM in a bookshop in Glebe. Mr Rudd didn't say much, but seemed pleasant enough.

Dan, Joe and Michael of One Ten Motorcycles, Caboolture, with Dorothy – the perfect bike for the trip. I wonder where Doris is now?

I'd camped in Longreach, Queensland, hitting the road at 4 a.m. A couple of hours of dark chill, then sunrise. I'd see maybe four cars in an hour.

Across the Outback I'd see the black clouds on the horizon. Ten minutes of downpour. Soaking. Ten minutes of sunshine. Dry again.

The road to Mount Isa. It was the wet season and road closures meant I didn't see many road trains crossing the Outback. This was a good thing as they really blow you about when they overtake.

It took two days to track Dot down once she'd landed in East Timor. I went from the docks to the offices of the shipping agency, then back to the docks before being bundled in a taxi and driven to this yard on the outskirts of Dili. It was great to see her.

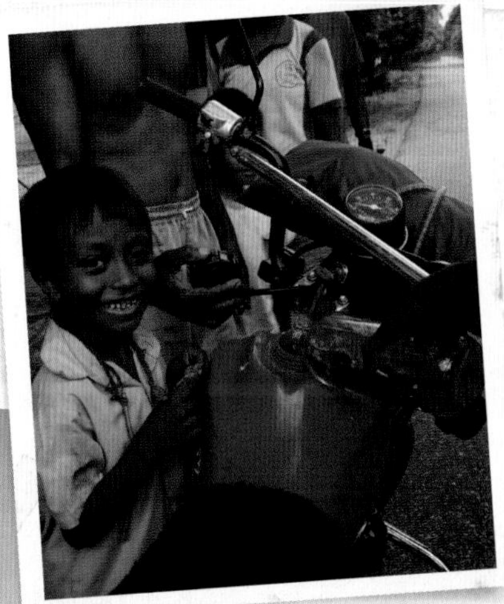

Across much of Indonesia, fuel was often sold like this, in glass bottles by the side of the road. It was so watered down it made Dot 'pop'.

Rice fields in Sumbawa, Indonesia. I'd been riding with Ethan, an eighteen-year-old from Alaska on a hired scooter from Bali. We got separated and I never saw him again.

In Bali I rode around the rim of the Agung volcano (above) before dropping down into its black rock crater, then headed to Kuta, the main tourist town, where a memorial (left) stands for those killed in the bombings of 2002 and 2005.

The BigZoners, an Indonesian biker gang I met in Sumatra. Their motto: 'Keep Brotherhood till Die'. Me and Dot are founding members of the English chapter. One day we'll go back to visit.

The moment I stopped being afraid and camped out in the Indonesian wild. Just me, the world and the thunderstorm.

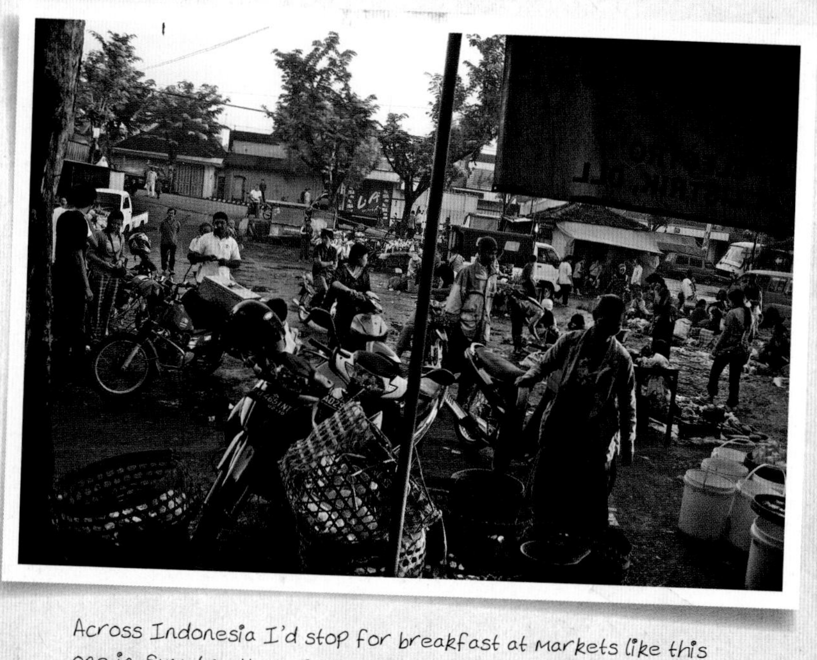

Across Indonesia I'd stop for breakfast at markets like this one in Sumatra. Here I ate chicken satay with locals who all followed English football.

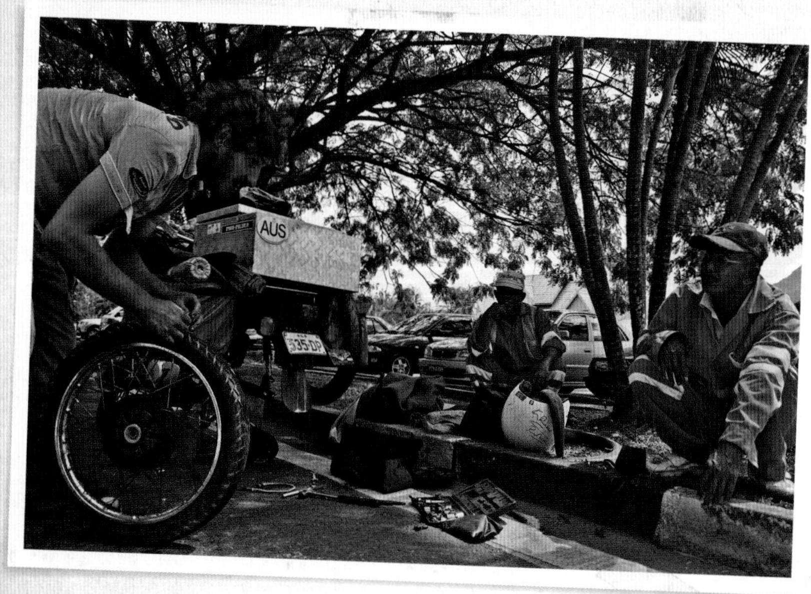

So many punctures, maybe twenty in total. This one happened in Malaysia, heading towards the Thai border. Some road workers watched me repair it.

I arrived in Bangkok just in time for Thai New Year (in April). While political rioting continued in parts of the capital, the rest of the city threw water over each other and smeared each other in clay. It's tradition.

The three of us – me, Mandy and Dol – on our way to the remote Treehouse II hostel in Ko Chang, Thailand. In hindsight, thongs were not suitable footwear.

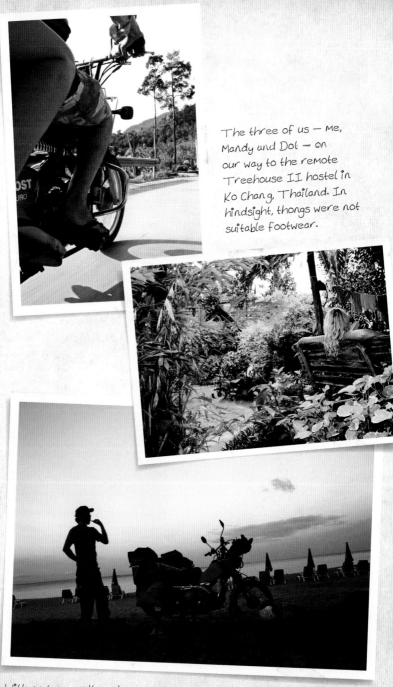

With no base or 'home' you can get caught out, not sure of what to do, or where to go. It's an odd sensation. This day I slept on Phuket beach.

Dodging buses in Nepal. You have to be alert and confident on foreign roads. I think that's why I struggled crossing the Indian border, My confidence had gone.

As a foreigner, it cost A$20 to get in to The Taj Mahal; locals pay less than one dollar. You have to wear socks over your shoes. It was OK, but I preferred the Hawaiian pizza I had nearby.

Bodies rot on the banks of the River Ganges as it flows through Varanasi, India. Locals will take you in boats to see them. It's strange — you should feel repulsed, but you don't. It's just the way of life.

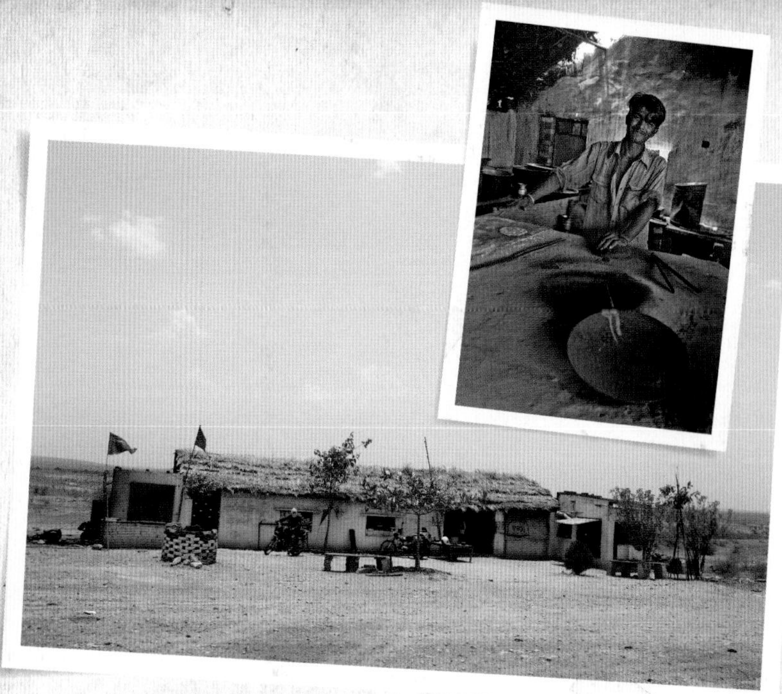

On the long hot road to Delhi, I was invited to eat here by two strangers. I was reluctant; I'd lost my trust in things. But it turned out to be a good day, and a good feast. Then back to the forty-eight degree heat.

Me with James and Nancy, who were touring India on a Royal Enfield, on the Manali to Leh Highway. Strangely, it was a popular thing to do for Israelis fresh out of national service. (PHOTO: NANCY KAISER)

Preparing for Pakistan. If Dot hadn't successfully made it through the Indian Himalayas on the Manali to Leh Highway, I would have had to fly us to Turkey. (PHOTO: NANCY KAISER)

I was helped by so many people along the way that it was hard not to believe in the 'fairies' Denise in Mt Isa had told me about. This is Sascha, the ginger-haired German I met on the highway to Leh.
(PHOTO: NANCY KAISER)

Supply trucks heading to Leh. Slow enough to overtake. Military trucks also use this road because of the Kashmir conflict. I considered putting Dot on one when she was struggling.

Top of the world in the Indian Himalayas, almost 5325 metres high. Ski resorts in Europe and Australia are often less than 2000 metres by comparison. Dot nearly died up here. (PHOTO: NANCY KAISER)

Michel on Dot and me on his BMW in a back alley in Lahore, Pakistan. He was staying at the same hostel while we waited for visas and was heading to India and Nepal before shipping his bike home to the Netherlands. I doubt I could have handled his bike.

Year round, teams of labourers repair the Karakoram Highway that connects Pakistan and China. Not far from here I met a bus-load of English people on a climbing tour of the Himalayas.

My helmet completely ruined my disguise in Pakistan as none of the locals wore them. My health insurance was void without one. No one was fooled, not even the cows.

Mystery horseman, Kyrgyzstan. He appeared from nowhere, had me sit on his horse, then wrote his address for me so I could send him a photo I'd taken. The address didn't make much sense so I never sent it.
If only I'd carried a Polaroid camera.

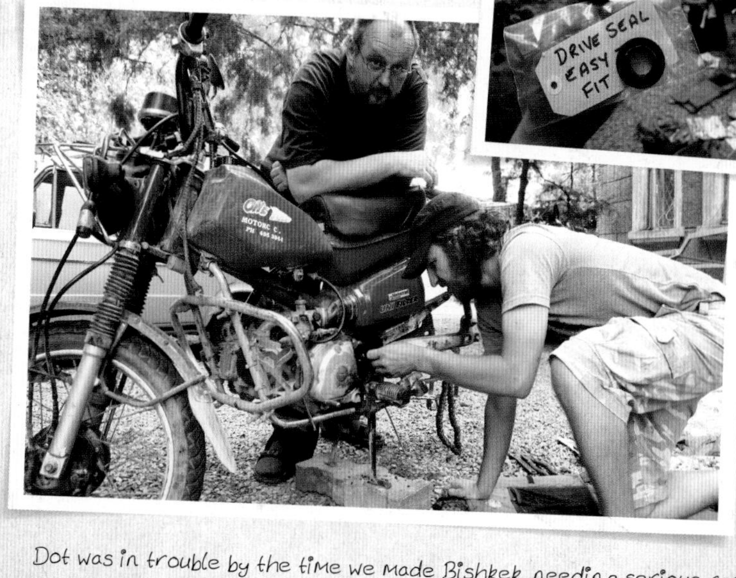

Dot was in trouble by the time we made Bishkek, needing serious repair. Had it not been for the Hülsmanns, not to mention Joe back in Caboolture who sent me some parts, I'd probably still be there. (PHOTO: CLAUDIA HÜLSMANN)

Travelling across Kazakhstan with the Hülsmanns really allowed me to relax; I could follow for a while, have someone watch my back and keep me company. Though while it was enjoyable for me, it must have been hard for them given their bikes could go so much faster.

(PHOTO: ANDREAS HÜLSMANN)

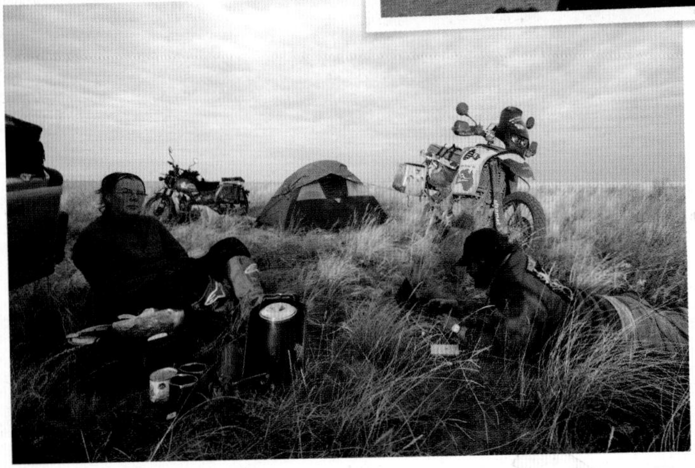

At night we'd pull off the road into the Steppe, pitch tents, boil some water, make tea, eat noodles and bread. This was taken the day Dot had some engine worries and with six thousand kilometres still to go, I was panicking. (PHOTO: ANDREAS HÜLSMANN)

Sleeping behind a Russian hedge, in the corner of a farmer's field. I was never spotted. Some mornings I didn't want to get out of the sleeping bag, but I had to.

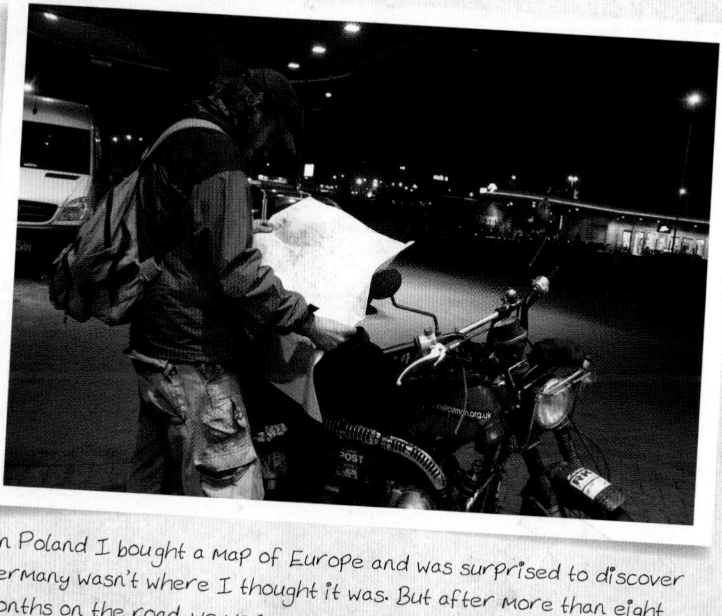

In Poland I bought a map of Europe and was surprised to discover Germany wasn't where I thought it was. But after more than eight months on the road, we were now on the home stretch.

Old and new friends greeted me and Dot in Dover. Some had followed our trip on the internet and came down to say hello. A big thank you to everyone who came.

A big shock for my parents getting an email saying I'm three days into a bike trip across the world. I next saw them nine months later. Mum gave me a bear hug which almost killed me.

Dot and the C90 I was originally going to do the trip on. I don't think it would have made it. Though New Zealander Ryan Scott rode a C50 from Vietnam to England.

banners beside them. It was a unique backdrop to Mandy's arrival. To think, the last time we saw each other was in Sydney, the day I rode away on a motorbike, her reflection gradually getting smaller in my rear-view mirror. That we'd somehow survived this long was a triumph, given the strain on things, and the way the idea for the trip was conceived.

We didn't really have a plan for her two-week stay. Mandy had been to Thailand several times before and having seen the beaches was keen to check out the more mountainous north, an area centred around Chiang Mai. Sadly, because of those darn protests, the trains had been cancelled, and after an evening spent sitting on the platform with a thousand other people waiting for them to resume, we gave up, returned to the guesthouse, slept, snored, cuddled, and in the morning woke up and had breakfast overlooking the square. We had lots to talk about, but catching up came first. And trimming my moustache, because it tickled her when we kissed.

We devised a plan to escape the city on the back of Dot, though not to Chiang Mai because it was too far away. In the opposite direction instead, down the coast, a day's ride, until we reached a point where we could get a ferry across to the island of Ko Chang. It would be more beaches, but that was okay. To make sure Dot could carry the pair of us properly, I stuffed her sheepskin seat cover with jumpers and used bungee cords to strap it to the rack on the back. Mandy could fill one pannier, while I had the other for tools and a few clothes. She would use my helmet, while I wore a plastic one bought from the supermarket for seven bucks. She would have to rest her feet on the pannier racks — now mended after the Indonesian bus — and hold on tight, though the other couple from Australia had already proven that you can ride a long way two-up on a postie bike. They were now in India. I admired them even more.

And then we set off, the three of us, me, Mandy and Dot, weaving through Bangkok city, getting lost and pulling up at busy junctions where we were the centre of attention. Thailand was by far my favourite place on the journey so far, and it was hard to imagine at this point how life could be any better. Astride a brilliant bike, in the middle of a great city, heading to the beach, with the girl who owned me on the back with her arms around me and her head resting on my shoulder, having flown all this way to visit me. If you could pause life and live in the same moment forever and ever — *Groundhog Day* — then this would be my moment. Though I did feel a little nervous having her on the back. It was the weight of responsibility. 'Whatever you do, don't crash,' I told myself as we struggled to keep up with the traffic on the freeway running southeast from the city.

One of the best things was how I'd long since taken all this for granted, a motorbike through a foreign land with no clue where I was going and every road and place a new one. It was my day job. I got up and did it without even thinking. Now I had someone who was new to the concept, they were excited by the possibilities of the endless road, and that made me buzz as well, which was a curious thing. Travelling for so long on my own I'd noticed how, after a while, I began to flat line, and cruise along emotionally neutral because there was no point in being happy or sad because there was no one there to witness it. Now it all came flooding back. Those arms tightening around my waist, the sun getting hotter, Mandy talking to me over my shoulder, asking me where we should eat, and how we're doing for petrol, and how long until we get there. We just needed a soundtack, maybe Canned Heat, *Going up the Country*.

In a city on the way we got caught up in the carnage of Songkran, the New Year festival involving water fights and clay being smeared on faces. It had been taking place across all of Thailand, even in Bangkok, just down from the protestors, though you wouldn't have seen it on the news. Youths in trucks now tried to drench us as we weaved through lanes of traffic that had been brought to a standstill. It's great for a day, all right for two, but this being the third day of celebrations I was keen to stay dry, so I tested Dot's agility, two-up, weaving between gaps in the traffic, all the while trying to use other vehicles as shields from the water that locals were determined to throw over the foreigners on the motorbike, for fun of course.

We made it to Pattaya, halfway to Ko Chang, staying the night in a hotel in the centre of this seedy beachside resort. We walked around that evening amazed at the sex scene and the number of local girls doing rude dances for the Western men who later would take them back to their hotel on rented scooters and perhaps to the embassy the next day. Despite the tropical surroundings, we rowed that night, just about the situation and where it went from here. It was more frustration than direct attack. Mandy, rightly, just wanted some certainty, about what was going to happen at the end, where we both might be. Normal questions that need to be asked. I struggled with them, because I had no answers.

I didn't know how much longer this journey was going to take; it was already taking much longer than I'd anticipated, even though I was doing it as quickly as I could. It was also difficult with Pakistan looming on the horizon. I struggled to see beyond it. I saw it as my nemesis, the one that I had to face and hope for relief at the other end. I was fatalistic, and also realistic. But knowing more than ever that I couldn't skip that stage, or turn away from it. In setting off I'd put myself on a path, and I felt I had to follow it all the way to the end, or else never know where it might take me. It didn't help that I was still riding away from her, and her life. The route, sadly, wasn't circular, unless I went full circle.

Catching the ferry to Ko Chang the next day we rode around the island to Lonely Beach, the quietest beach. We stayed there well over a week, doing nothing in particular, just swimming and eating cheap food beneath a huge pagoda overlooking the sea, sitting on cushions, relaxing with a cold drink. Mandy had brought me a tube of Vegemite and so we had that on toast every morning with a cup of tea. We were staying in bungalows right on the beachfront. They were on stilts and consisted of just one square room, with a bed in the middle with a mosquito net overhead and a partition wall with a shower and toilet behind. For safekeeping, I hung my SLR camera on the back of the shower door, went for a swim, came back, had a shower, forgot about the camera. And it never worked again.

Later we got drunk, which was the worst feeling in the world because all this way I'd needed to be totally alert and watchful for everything, in front of me and behind; I had to be. Now I couldn't sit up straight or see properly, and the sense of vulnerability scared me. I didn't drink after that. In the nights that followed we sat on the bungalow steps, listening to the sound of the crashing waves in the darkness, Mandy telling me about the things I was missing: our friends who were getting married, the parties they'd had in the back garden, the days in the park, the movies she'd watched, the good times she'd had, in Sydney, a place I still, deep down, considered my home. I missed it more than ever now. I looked at the reality of where I'd been the last four months, in dirty hotels, in danger, fourteen-hour days on the road. You think the world waits for you while you do these things; it doesn't, it moves on.

Despite my need to finish the trip, we talked about me flying back to Sydney with her instead. There was a chance I could get another tourist visa and start again, try again. Who knows, maybe with better luck, and greater conviction, something good will happen, and I will find a way to stay. I thought about it, abandoning Dorothy, out here, in Thailand, and flying back with Mandy. But I was scared. What if it didn't work out, what if I ended up in the café again, waiting to be kicked out? And if I did get a permanent job, with sponsorship, would I resent Mandy for being the reason I never finished what I started? Irrational, perhaps, but at the time I told myself that I needed to finish this if it was ever going to work between us two. Why I thought this trip was the answer to all this I'm now, with hindsight, not quite sure. It had become my obsession, to reach England.

We headed back to Bangkok on the eve of Mandy's flight home. She took the bus because I had to detour down to the border with Cambodia to renew Dot's temporary import slip as it expired in a few days and I didn't want to be landed with that huge fine. Mandy then would arrive in Bangkok before me, returning to the same guesthouse we stayed at before. I was on the road all day, playing catch-up, racing as hard as I could, excited, because I knew that when I opened the guesthouse door that evening there would be Mandy, lying on the bed, or in the shower, or ready to go for dinner. And that was just the best feeling. The best of the whole trip, because in this crazy world of motorbikes and roads across the world, this was a taste of normality, of how life should be. And could be. If only I had the nerve, and the will, to abandon this and go back and try again. I couldn't.

Saying goodbye at the airport the next day was horrid. I got a taste of what it felt like to be the one being left behind. It was as if the roles had been reversed and I was being left to my routine while Mandy went off and lived the exciting life. And now, as I stood against the glass partition at Bangkok airport watching Mandy go through Customs and security, turn and wave and then disappear from sight, I felt the very uneasy sensation that this would be the last time I would see her. I caught the bus back into the centre of Bangkok, looking out the window at that familiar skyline, thinking of the journey ahead and the events that had just taken place. I can't begin to imagine what Mandy must have been thinking up in the air, staring out the aeroplane window, looking down at the same skyline as it slowly disappeared from view, perhaps thinking it's finally time she got on with her own life, and moved on.

A week later, she did.

13

Up and Over

Somewhere

There's a problem with riding from Sydney to London on a motorbike. And that problem is Burma, or Myanmar as it's officially known. A military dictatorship, the country doesn't allow foreigners to pass through it, either on foot or by bike. You can fly into Rangoon, the capital, or cross the border for the day, but you can't enter one end and leave the other. That leaves you two options: either go up and over through China and back down into Nepal and India, or you put your bike on a plane and fly over, usually to Nepal, though some go to Bangladesh, as the other guys on the postie had just done. You'd think riding through China would be the cheapest option, but with the government insisting that foreign vehicles be escorted at all times by a guide — costing as much as $200 a day — it was actually much cheaper to put her on an aeroplane and fly her to Kathmandu, the capital of Nepal.

It had been an easier process than I had anticipated. I simply found a freighting agent in Bangkok, got a few quotes, told them where and when I wanted Dot to go, filled in some paperwork and then, a few days before the flight, took her down to the depot to have a wooden crate built around her. I'd read in advance that to save money the trick is to make your bike as tiny as possible; that way the box is smaller and so is the cost. With that in mind I stripped her of the handlebars, pannier racks, foot pegs, engine guard and even her front wheel until she was no bigger than a bicycle. It had cost around 500 bucks, with all the removed parts squeezed down the gaps inside the wooden box.

The sky the night I flew to Kathmandu was menacing, full of thunder and rage. I sat by the window and watched the violent streaks of lightning tear a hole in the purple haze. The rays of sunlight were streaking through the clouds I could see down below. It was an epic sight, a reminder that up here we're not in charge, we're just bodies in metal tubes suspended in the sky, and if we were to fall from it that night, in the grand scheme of things, it wouldn't be such a big deal. I wasn't then so afraid of flying tonight. Perhaps now, after the separation that had just occurred, I found solace in my acceptance that you can never have done enough, been enough, seen enough. Lived enough. There will always be something to chase. And in a strange way, I found contentment in this, and also tears. I guess this was the reality of life, not just flying.

* * *

At the airport in Kathmandu I was directed to the cargo depot along from the main terminal. The Himalayas rose all around us — an entirely new landscape for me. While an official set about finding Dot's crate, I sat next to an old man who seemed totally disgruntled that I was there, in his country. 'What are you doing here?' he barked with no concern for how or if I answered. By now I was used to being the odd one out, but when the lights are so dim and every other face is brown you feel a bit apologetic about your big white head sticking out. But most of them didn't care; they were just curious, and a huge crowd gathered around when I was finally presented with a slender wooden crate that didn't seem big enough for a motorbike at all.

A man with a crowbar began levering at the lid, forcing the wood away from the nails as if he were opening some ancient artefact discovered in a tomb. I stood trying to figure it out. I was in a warehouse in Nepal — a country I had no clue about apart from what I'd heard from other people I'd met along the way — collecting a bike I'd ridden from Sydney, and with a stamp in my passport for Pakistan. It didn't feel real at all, though, of course, it was very real — I could smell the thick cigarette-laden atmosphere and see the chaotic world I'd ridden from Australia to find. Then the drums flared, fireworks exploded, trumpets roared, and there, amidst the crowd at Kathmandu air cargo terminal, Colin's old motorbike stole its first breath of Nepalese air.

She was wrapped head to toe in clingfilm and mounted on a strong wooden base. Curious faces asked questions about power and price — low on both counts, of course — but still she drew a crowd. With the assistance of two strangers I lifted her from the base, setting her down on the floor and gathering together all the pieces I'd removed in Bangkok. As I laid out the tools and bolts to put her back together, a dozen hands reached in and took them, though not to steal; they just wanted to help and I couldn't have stopped them if I'd tried. In no time at all the handlebars, front wheel, foot pegs and engine guard were all bolted back on, and there Dot stood, in this hangar, surrounded by Nepalese. I emptied petrol from two soft drink bottles into her tank and rolled her out into the sunlight.

I was joined by the crowd, jostling and excited. There was a big open loading space in front of the hangar. If I looked to my left I could see the skyline of nearby Kathmandu, with its Himalayan backdrop — the city in the sky. I would be heading there soon. I turned the key. The green light glowed. I pulled out the kickstand and placed the sole of my right boot on it. I steadied myself, thought positive thoughts, and then …

Kick … kick … kick … and kick … Nothing.

She just would not start. In a way I felt she was playing to the crowd, making me look a fool for her amusement and that she'd only start in her own good time. This went on for five minutes or more, just pumping and pumping, until the crowd motioned for me to put my feet on the pegs and hold on tight — they were going to give me a bump start.

I'd been reading *Zen and the Art of Motorcycle Maintenance*. It tells the story of a guy who's had a nervous breakdown and rediscovers his past on the back of his motorbike. It's a book I liked very much, except for the bit where the author defines his bike as nothing but an assembly of metal and bolts, governed entirely by science and reason. In the early stages of the trip I might have agreed, but now, having come so far, I was convinced I could feel Dot ageing, finding the best way to cope with the difficult conditions, just like me. That's why I had to believe those farts and whistles and bad days she had weren't caused by the air mixture or something else rational, but were instead the result of her mood or her period or other things unfathomably female. And so …

Down the ramp we sailed, neutral now, then first, right fist to the gutter, a cough and a splutter. And there, in the warm afternoon sun, she lived.

14

Footprints

Kathmandu

Flying into Nepal marked the point of no return, as I had effectively posted myself into a trap. Behind me was Burma, ahead lay India and Pakistan, but I had no certain way yet of being allowed further than that. To fly here without an Iranian visa, knowing how hard it was to get one, was probably my biggest gamble, but one I felt I had to take just to keep the wheels moving. And I liked movement, especially now; it took my mind off things, allowing no time to look over my shoulder, only ahead, at what needed to be done. I knew if I stopped now I would be in trouble, the wheels grinding to a halt and the dogs snapping at my heels; maybe Adi was lurking nearby as well. That's why I'd pushed on, to Nepal, to figure it all out from here.

Now I was riding into the centre of Kathmandu, a place described to me so many times by the people I'd met on the journey, yet their words could not do justice to the pandemonium I encountered for myself. The city sits high, in a nest of snow-capped mountains, with crumbling buildings that for all the world looked like victims of war, granddad structures with stories to tell and sagging lungs that exhaled with a wheeze when the wind blew fierce. A bit like the talking trees in *Lord of the Rings* if that makes more sense. I rode between them, dodging the flood of oncoming motorcycles as I went, realising as I did so that a flight over Burma doesn't just bring you to a different country but to a different world.

In fact I'd been advised not to fly here, to fly to Bangladesh instead, as at times in the past the petrol pumps in Kathmandu have run dry, a consequence of ongoing political turmoil. You could sense the instability in the atmosphere, in the faces and the mood of the million souls who live amongst those crumbling structures, almost as though it was the calm before the next storm. Roadblocks were commonplace, as were riots. Yet it was a fascinating world, full of colour and movement, a maze of lanes, dark and eerie, offering a glimpse beneath the rim of society, like a Terry Pratchett novel come alive.

This was the tourist district, Thamel, where hippy travellers get stoned and mountaineers make preparations for climbing the peaks all around. Kids would try and sell them drugs as they wandered about. Children as young as ten, some barefoot, stood on corners taking a deep lung full of some substance from clear plastic bags, which made them sway, their eyes completely glazed. They were cheeky, persistent and bothersome. You'd tell them to go away, but they'd follow you until you darted into one of the many shops to take a moment's peace from the street, which by 10 p.m. was almost empty. A sinister air then descended on the place, the shadows seemingly chasing you from the bar back to your bedroom. I made sure I knew which pocket the knife was in.

In a way, Thailand had lulled me into a false sense of belief in my confidence and composure. I felt I knew the world there and began to relax and not worry about danger. But here in Kathmandu I once more felt out of my depth, uncertain, nervous, as though I had to learn it all again. I'd not expected this and it took a few days in Kathmandu to feel comfortable and able to deal with the people who hassled me, as many people did. I was morose at this point, which I think didn't help, but I had to get a grip and very quickly locate that person who'd slept rough in the Indonesian wild, who'd ridden through the Thai night, because right now I was back in East Timor airport, with my head in my hands, and that would be a dangerous state of mind for surviving in this world, and the Indian one below it.

My immediate concern, however, was the cancellation of my debit card after someone in Poland had managed to hack into my account and steal some money — not much, but enough to alert the bank and have them shut all my accounts down. Having only ten dollars in my wallet at the time was quite a problem, but my parents, as incredible as ever, came to the rescue, and wired me through some money. This was necessary as Dot would need oil and a new rear tyre before she could be ridden any further. The owner of the guesthouse directed me to a bike shop not far away. It was just a small place, on the side of a busy street. Inside was that familiar smell of oil and leather, and a range of exciting gadgets and accessories, strewn across the walls and floor.

I talked motorbikes with the shopkeeper as he serviced Dot and changed the tyre. He was a curious stranger, asking about my trip and how I was paying for it. He didn't seem too fazed when I told him of my credit card debt, explaining how it was all that I had when faced with the sudden opportunity to set off. He'd met other bikers like me, and was excited about seeing Dot as they used to sell the same model here, in Nepal; in fact he used to own one. We chatted a while. Then, as I was about to leave, he asked me where my waterproof riding gear was. 'I don't have any,' I replied, cursing the day I'd posted home those given to me by the BigZoners in the belief it wouldn't rain west of Thailand. Of course it had already and was also quite cold. I'd resigned myself to managing with what I had.

'Wait there then,' he said, darting back into his shop and emerging a minute later with a salmon pink waterproof jacket and matching trousers. 'I want you to have these,' he said, passing them to me and indicating that I was to try them on. I did so in the street, beside the busy road, the old king's palace in the distance at the end. The wet-weather gear was a perfect fit, and the colour was quite unique. I said, 'Thank you', and deeply meant it because I knew just how much I would need them. Though in a way, given the nature of things, I didn't quite feel as though I deserved them.

RUSSIA
KAZAKHSTAN
10 DAYS
CASPIAN SEA
TURKEY
TURKMENISTAN
IRAN
IRAQ
AFGHANISTAN
KKH
PAKISTAN
1 WEEK
SAUDI ARABIA
KYRGYZSTAN
3 WEEKS
CHINA
1 WEEK
2 WEEKS
NEPAL
INDIA
2 MONTHS
MYANMAR (BURMA)
THAILAND
1. THAILAND
2 KATHMANDU
3 POKHARA
4 VARANASI
5 AGRA (TAJ MAHAL)
6 DELHI
7 MANALI
8. LEH
9. LAHORE
10. ISLAMABAD
11. KASHGAR
12 OSH
13. BISHKEK
14 SHYMKENT
= FLIGHT PATH
- - - INTENDED ROUTE
— ROUTE TAKEN

It was a strange time. I had to push on to India, to sort out visas and clear the road ahead. But at the same time I wanted a break from all this, from riding, from Dot, from this world of motorbikes and long roads. Escape from escaping. So, inspired by the sight of all the climbers around, I thought I would take to the mountains myself. In Kathmandu I'd met three other travellers, a Frenchman called Nicolas and two girls, who were keen to go walking as well. We looked at the options as we sat in the guesthouse garden, behind a big metal gate. We could either hire one of the local guides and pay for mules and porters, the cost high, or we could pay a few dollars for a permit and go off on our own with a map. Plenty of people did it this way. We chose the latter, deciding on the Annapurna Circuit.

This is 259 kilometres in length, peaking at a height of 5416 metres. It should take around two to three weeks — perfect. I left Dot at a guesthouse at the bottom, beneath a tarp, in the back yard. From there the trail began. A footbridge across a river, then left and along the water's edge as it began to work its way up the valley. The greenery here was lush, a mixture of crops and grassy expanses, criss-crossed by meandering streams with stepping stones. Occasionally, we'd meet a local walking the other way. Slowly the path began to steepen, with steps of rock and loose shale that at times would require a hand to help you up and a good pump from the calf muscles that were now under considerable strain. It was like climbing those steps of the Tiger Temple all over again. We had to walk nine hours a day if we were going to cover the circuit in the recommended time.

The villages we passed through, accessible only by foot, hung off the edge of cliffs or were buried deep in the rock. Straw on the stone floor, hand pumps for water, animals in pens, old men sitting on steps. They all had little snack stalls selling water and chocolate, the price of which rose with the altitude. In the peak season of October and November the trail would have been packed, but now in May, being very much the low season, we were almost the only walkers, so accommodation in the little wooden guesthouses along the way was free if you ate lunch and dinner there. The showers were freezing, the rooms bare, but to wake up in a place overlooking a gorgeous waterfall halfway up a Nepalese mountain is surely worth a little suffering.

Though what would I know about that? On one particular steep and craggy climb we watched a group of men carrying building materials in big sacks, the straps strung across their heads, their necks straining, only able to take a few steps before having to rest. They did this in shorts and rubber sandals, and resembled a line of ants, as they slowly made their way to the town of Manang, 3500 metres above sea level, and not accessible by road. We were told it took them two weeks to get there, and for that they were paid quite well in Nepalese terms. I'm not surprised. In this modern age it all seemed so mystifying to see this way of life, carrying everything needed to sustain a town in the clouds. I imagine nothing had changed for hundreds, if not thousands, of years.

I just wish my mind had been better in tune with what was around. The further I walked, the steeper the terrain became, the more I realised that, actually, this wasn't for me. I shouldn't have come. I already had my challenge and had neither the endurance nor patience to take on another one. More than ever I just wanted to get to England, to see if I could. And being out here, on this mountain, wasn't achieving that, it was wasting time and energy; at least that's how I saw it at the time. I thought how I could be in Delhi already, sorting out my visa for Iran. Then I worried about Dot. I'd callously abandoned the bike that had brought me all this way. And if she was stolen or vandalised, then I saw how all of this would have been in vain. Pointless, and then I would be left with nothing. Besides, as I already knew from my motorcycle trip, the further you venture, the harder it is to turn back.

On the evening of day two I explained to the others that the Annapurna Circuit wasn't for me, then woke early the next morning and set off back the way I'd come. I was so desperate to get to the bottom of the mountain that I covered the distance in just nine hours, nearly running most of the way. It was a great relief to find Dot where I'd left her, in the back yard of the guesthouse. She was under a sheet, up against a wall. After retrieving the aluminium box from the manager's office and bolting it back on, I considered staying the night as it was already early evening. But I couldn't bear to sit still. I had to get going, make up for lost time and ride as fast as I could.

So off we set, me and Colin's old motorbike, heading west in the direction of Pokhara, Nepal's second city, some three hours away. It was a murderous road, weaving down mountains and out along the valley floor. Once the light had gone I could barely see a thing, only the shadows and the subtle outline of people, who just seemed to meander onto the road. They didn't care that a motorcycle was howling past, dodging the potholes, ridden by a man possessed, his visor open for extra visibility. I felt the first flicks of rain, then sheets of it began to pound down, until I would have been drenched had it not been for my new riding suit given to me by a stranger; if only he knew. At 10 p.m. I reached Pokhara, finding a hotel by the lake, where I woke the following morning with diarrhoea so bad I couldn't leave the room for a week. The absence of movement just about finished me. Though I had plenty of movement of the other kind.

15

Dead in the Water

Indian Border

The road to the Indian border was the hardest of them all. Not because it was too steep or badly surfaced, though it was both, but because I just didn't want to be there. The feeling was one of guilt, for being out here, for doing this, for not finding a way to stay in Sydney, for not going back, for having my parents worry, for taking Mandy for granted. It was other things as well, like hearing my nan hadn't been so well — nothing serious, but weakening, through age, Mum updating me on her condition and me feeling as though I should be there, how that should be my priority, not this stupid adventure. Such a thing had happened before, the first time I was in Australia, when Granddad Stan had died and I wasn't there, neither for the final moments nor the funeral. You convince yourself you can't be there, that you have to live your own life. Then you think about other people's needs and feel utterly selfish.

The prospect of riding 15,000 kilometres, through places

such as India and Pakistan, now filled me with dread. I thought about flying back to Australia to try and make amends, I thought about flying to England. But I couldn't bring myself to do either. I couldn't make that decision. I took the easiest one. I carried on, riding through the south of Nepal, through the valleys and the villages, where people looked forlorn as they walked by the side of the road, and hardly ever met my eye. Maybe it was my mood or the unsettled political situation, but of all the places I'd ridden Nepal was the one where I sensed it wouldn't be a good place to break down. Not because I thought I might be in danger; more likely that I wouldn't be helped.

It was late in the afternoon when I made the final approach to the border, the road lined with a thousand trucks, all parked bumper to bumper. I don't know if they were waiting to cross or whether they were *just* waiting. I rode past them trying to psyche myself up; 'COME ON,' I forced through gritted teeth. Some of the stories I'd heard about riding in India were horrific. Apparently, with the way the Indian compensation system works, if you are struck by a vehicle once, you are likely to be struck twice to make sure you are dead, because the fine for killing someone on the road is less than if you maim them.

I couldn't cross the border. I just couldn't do it. I was too frightened. I turned around and began riding back the way I'd come, back into Nepal. It was perhaps now 5 p.m. and I just didn't know what to do, my indecisiveness had returned. I had another go at the border, getting close to it and then turning back again. I just could not bring myself to cross it, though I knew I would have to; just not tonight. I headed instead to the little town of Lumbini, apparently the birthplace of Buddha, which I knew was maybe forty kilometres down a road running parallel to the border. It was a dusty, dark, truck-infested road.

The town consisted of one dishevelled street that was dark and eerily silent. Being on the tourist map for its temples and monasteries, Lumbini had a scattering of guesthouses on either side of the road. I chose one that would allow me to roll Dot inside reception. The bedroom was on the first floor and filthy, the sheets seemingly not changed for months. I laid the wicker mat from East Timor and the sarong I'd bought in Bali on the bed as a base cover and went out, across the road, to a restaurant still serving food. On the balcony I talked to some travellers about Iranian visas. By coincidence most of them had tried to get one, or knew someone else who had, and all had failed. The simple truth is that the Iranians don't like the British, thanks to our meddling with their politics in the past. Not being able to get a visa would be a huge problem for me, because Iran was on my route to England.

The next morning I woke still not wanting to cross the border but knowing I had no choice. I rolled Dot out onto the dusty street, slugging back a chai from a stall by the road, then on we went, zapping past those lorries and finally succeeding in making it to the border, where an officious Customs officer made life hell. Things were photocopied, and I had to run between buildings in the blazing sun, all the while my bowels feeling like they were about to explode, bunged up on

Imodium, the flood gates about to break. I was relieved, but not in that sense, when finally I could pass beneath the arch marking the border.

A metre into India I was ordered to stop beside a desk and dismount, presenting my passport and visa to a man in the shadows. The world around me was chaos. He pointed me to the Customs house across the crowded road. I dodged lorries and cycles to get there, bursting through the door and into a long narrow room. A man in military uniform addressed me in English. He asked about the nature of my business. I told him I wanted to ride across his land and into Pakistan. He looked incredulous. I looked incredulous. He opened a giant tome of data, a storehouse of information on all machines that had passed this point in all years past. Dot's details were now entered, making a record of this moment until the end of time. This was 2 June 2009; we had covered almost 18,000 kilometres and it was our 142nd day on the road.

And what a road now, spearing south of the border, Nepal disappearing behind us, the barren hot land of India sprawling out ahead, because for once the man-made divide meant something to nature as well. This was the point at which the moist foothills of the Himalayas levelled out and shot flat and straight with barely a single thing growing from the earth. The air was immediately hotter and drier. The colour of the world was monotone, almost a dusty red in whichever direction you turned. I didn't imagine this openness, this vastness of India. But I wasn't surprised to see evidence of the road toll I'd heard about — the wreckage of vehicles littered the roadsides. In one place, two lorries had collided head on, their cabins evaporated. There was death in that, had to be.

But stopping for my first snack warmed me to the people. It was a stall serving food and quickly my visit drew an observant crowd. Children from the village came swarming, standing around curious about everything I owned, especially my helmet camera which was now strapped on with tape since the clips had broken. I sat at a table, all eyes on me. This was like being back in the deepest depths of Indonesia again, just mingling, hanging out, trying to explain myself and tasting the local food, which was good. Especially the tea, or chai as they call it, sweet and hot. One kid invited me to look around his village, but I said no, and regretted it immediately when I saw his hurt expression.

Then my first city, Gorakhpur. More chaos. Policemen in khaki uniforms with chubby bellies, thick black moustaches and big sticks tried their best to impose order on the swarm of vehicles, but they couldn't even control the sacred cows wandering the streets, chewing on the urban crud that gathered in the gutter and gives the sense that the city rose from a landfill. But that's just the Indian way. That's why some love it, some hate it. At times I would feel both emotions. Sometimes I wished my horn operated rockets so I could blow other drivers off the road when they came right at me. Other times I thought it so crazy I *had* to like it. This is a world that doesn't exist anywhere else. It is unique, and magical for being that way.

As for riding in an Indian city, you just had to let yourself go and feel the flow of the traffic — bend with it, don't fight it — like thousands of droplets of water all trying to make it down the same narrow rock face. I pulled up outside one shop completely lost. I was looking for a hotel, but in the swarm I couldn't find one. A man on a motorbike introduced himself and offered to help. Away he went, leading me down the back alleys and through the rancid streets to a place he knew, almost a copy of the White House, but one that hadn't been maintained for many years. That night I ate in a restaurant behind a baker's, the eyes of the other diners fixed on the man so rude as to enter such a place in cap and shorts. Etiquette — I'd lost all sense of that. I thought about trying to blend in by buying myself some new clothes at one of the many fabric shops that stayed open well into the night, but when it came to money I was now down to spending vapour.

Eventually that southerly road led me to Varanasi, a place where bodies are burnt on the banks of the River Ganges, the hope being that the souls go off to a better place. I stood and watched a funeral pyre — a pair of feet and a face blackened and charred and then turned to ashes. Then the area was raked flat for the space to be cleared and another fire to be lit and another body to be brought down to the water's edge, carried on the shoulders of the male family members, females not invited, and then burned until it was completely gone. This took place on a square of cascading steps not much bigger than a tennis court, six bodies burning at a time, those sacred cows still hanging around; no smell, surprisingly, just the constant bark of fraudsters trying to trick you into giving huge donations for poor families to buy the wood to burn the bodies, when often the fuel's provided free.

Every time I stepped from the guesthouse door I could guarantee that someone would be there to try and flog me drugs or clothes or postcards. And 'no' never meant 'no', not here. 'No' meant 'maybe', so all the way along the river's edge I would be followed until I'd get really mad and tell them to go away. And then I'd feel bad, because all this way I'd been conscious how as a traveller you are an ambassador for all other travellers, and the impression you leave affects how locals respond to the next person to pass through. That's why it really riled me to see people being rude to locals. It sets a bad precedent. And yet here I was, in India, telling someone to 'fuck off'. One guy who tried to rip me off defended himself by saying, 'You can't blame us for trying.' I agreed and responded, 'You can't blame us for getting pissed off when you do.'

The river was also used as the local bathtub, the residents of the city immersed in its murky waters by 5 a.m., bathing, scrubbing their laundry and teaching their children how to swim. To see a man gargle the green soupy water was enough to make you retch until you considered that it was you who'd got up at four o'clock that morning to hire a man with a boat to row you out to take the perfect picture of it all. Imagine opening your shower curtain every morning and finding a different stranger taking a picture of you in your undies, and that's how they must feel.

Often on these boat rides you would bump into a dead body floating on the surface. This was to be expected. Hindus believe that if you die from a cobra bite, or as a child, or from leprosy, or while pregnant, or as a holy man, you are already deemed 'pure' and therefore do not need to be cremated. Instead, the body is wrapped in fabric and rolled into the same stretch of river in which the living gargle and swim. It's an amazing scene, more so if you pay the oarsman to take you over to the other bank, a sandy beach, where those bodies wash up to be eaten by wild dogs. You can get as close to a decomposing body as you like, even pick up a skull or trip over a rib cage sticking up from the sand. And then you get the boat back and have your dinner of vegetable dosas sitting on a wooden bench.

I gave the boys who brought over the food a couple of extra rupees, a tip, and could see in their father's eyes he didn't appreciate that. What I think I'd inadvertently done was to demonstrate to his two sons that no matter how hard their father works the white man will always be richer. And they will always be poorer. As a result, it wasn't resentment or hatred he looked at me with, something else, I'm not sure what. A sense of lower worth? I hope not, because if there's one thing I will say about the people of India is that they're a resourceful bunch, working all hours of the day and well into the night seemingly with little interference or assistance from their government.

One day down by the river I met yet another Frenchman, this one named Bernard, who told me an amazing story about how he'd spent the last three months walking the length and breadth of southern India. No buses, no cars, nothing, just his own two feet. He lived on a dollar a day, sleeping by the side of the road, ostracised even by the Indians for being too poor. He was an interesting soul, on a journey, one he said was now complete, and he was ready to go home. His flight was leaving at the end of the week. I was jealous; to think I could be home in nine hours as well, as simple as getting on a plane. I couldn't, for fear of what that would leave me with; nothing.

I threatened to send many emails to Mandy trying to explain, trying to make amends, but by now she'd told me she needed a break completely and that I wasn't to contact her at all. And so I didn't, because I had no answers, no solutions to all this. So I saved my emails in 'draft', before heading back to the street in the forty-eight-degree heat, slowly falling into a trap of not being able to bring myself to leave this place, always having an excuse not to move on to the next. My enthusiasm for everything, for all *this*, was in the gutter, sailing by, being chewed up and digested by the holy cows until it drizzled out into the Ganges and was flushed completely away.

It took me ten days to escape Varanasi. I even tried putting Dot on the train so as to avoid 1000 kilometres of dangerous road between here and Delhi. I got as far as buying a ticket at the station and draining Dot of her fuel as instructed. But then I was told I would have to strip her completely bare of all her panniers and the aluminium box and I just couldn't be bothered, especially not as I'd have to carry it all on board with me. Besides, I set out to ride across the world, not to take lifts. So I snatched my fuel back from the vulture I'd given it to, poured it back into the tank, and fought to keep my place in the queue at the refund counter. It was a hot, sweaty, physical scrum. The counter was the ball.

Then, finally, the road to Delhi. I hit it with an urgency to find out once and for all if I could get an Iranian visa at the embassy. *Come on, pick yourself up. Enjoy this moment. I'm trying. I want to. But this is hard.* I felt the urge just to get there, to England, to be done with this, as unappreciative as that may be of the life I was living — I simply wanted it over. I'd ridden enough, I'd seen enough. I just wanted to go home. But for now, I had to survive this road, this long, dusty, dangerous road, on which trucks and buses didn't give a shit if we were there or not and would force us into the dirt. I'd curse at them as they passed, but might is right in India, you learn that very fast.

And in a strange way I enjoyed that road, the highlight not being the Taj Mahal, as impressive as that was the day I stopped in Agra, or the giant Hawaiian I had all to myself in the nearby Pizza Hut. Instead it was the moment in the middle of nowhere when I was disturbed from my toilet break in the bushes by a pair of local men who pulled up on a motorbike and greeted me like old friends. They brought their hands to their mouths to question if I was hungry. I wasn't at the most trusting point in the trip, but I thought what the hell, why not? I followed them for several kilometres until we pulled up outside what appeared to be a decrepit old cow shed. There was no door, no windows and the roof was in tatters. This didn't look like much of a café.

I dismounted with care, checking my knife was still in my pocket, ready to go. My friends were eager to lead me through the non-existent door and into a room illuminated by the patchwork of holes in the roof. Before me were eight beds, all steel and shy of mattresses. Lying on them were men who looked weary and hot and bothered, one a holy man dressed in orange robes, and smoking, yet they smiled and nodded a greeting as I walked through the door with my Kevin Rudd-inscribed helmet still on my head. Who they were I'm not entirely sure, but I suspected this to be a drop-in centre for vagrants and drifters making their way along this desolate dusty road. An oasis, run by a quizzical old man, in glasses, who must welcome the men as they wander past.

In the corner was a young man with a big smile who cooked fresh food in huge pans on a red-hot kiln. I had one portion, then another and still more came. It was a *thali* with rice and chapatti. I even drank the water from the well, which I didn't think I should do, but what the hell. This was an experience I needed because, rightly or wrongly, I'd developed quite a negative impression of India and of Indians. Too many had tried to trick me to think anything else, although this impression could have been a consequence of my mood. This, though, was a timely reminder that there are plenty of good folk out there, even if sometimes you have to travel further to find them. When I offered to pay, the man wouldn't dream of it. I thanked them all, and carried on my way. A great memory: the day I became an Indian drifter on the long dusty road to Delhi.

16

Change of Plan

Delhi

The backpacker zone of Paharganj was exactly where the map said it was, right at the heart of Delhi, opposite the train station where people arriving for the first time would be told they needed to take a tuk-tuk and so jumped in and rode around for half an hour before being dropped off a hundred metres down the road from where they originally got in. A popular scam and symbolic of the place you were about to enter. One long corridor of pedlars, meddlers, bandits and vagabonds, stretching a kilometre or more in length and lined with shops and food stalls and cows that you must swerve around as you ride at slow speed along the dusty street.

Dark alleyways lead off in every direction, the buildings leaning in at the top to trap you if ever tried to fly away. Hostels are scattered amongst them. Creepy places, with no place safe to leave your bike except chained to a gate, which is what I had to do with Dot, leaving her to choke on an air of stale piss, contributed by the men using the open urinals lashed to the side of the streets. You can walk past and pat the pisser on the back if you like; just hope they don't spin around and shoot *you* in the back. A dirt and rock floor covers it all, so when it rains the whole place turns to mud and makes your trousers brown.

There was one poor guy I kept seeing, Swedish going by his appearance, who was totally off his face on drugs. He had sores all over his arms and sat rocking on the pavement. He was a mess and I dread to think what happened to him. This place takes no prisoners and I suspect at some point he would have been circled like a pack of wolves and torn to shreds. I thought about helping him, but was too concerned for my own survival to really care. And so I stepped around him and left him in the gutter.

I ate in the cafés with their torn filthy fake tile floors, broken seats, chipped tables and vats of food at the front slopped into metal trays. The food was always good, and cheap, less than a buck. Outside I'd buy a kilo of mangoes at one of the wooden stalls and guard myself against the pickpockets. Three boys working together: one walks across your path and stops, which makes you stop; a second boy comes from behind and goes for your wallet while you're momentarily distracted, and stationary. If successful, he passes it to the third boy coming in the opposite direction. I felt the second boy go for my wallet and reacted. I thought about grabbing him and taking him to the police, but they would have beaten him black and blue. I carried on.

Watch the water. So many of the bottles had a small hole in the bottom that looked to have been resealed with heat to leave a messy plastic scar. Fake water, probably, but how? If they were refilling bottles already used then the seal on the cap would have been broken, and yet these 'fake' bottles had a seal, so if they could re-create a seal why the need for the hole? And if they couldn't re-create a seal what were they doing with the original water they drained out of the crude holes they were making in the bottom of the bottle? Drinking it themselves, flushing it down the loo? We didn't get it, help us out, we need those kids from *Scooby Doo*. They'll still be in Australia, solving the mystery of the caretaker croc.

Funny that. Every country and group of people I'd met along the way had a story to tell about the danger in their own back yard. Or in their neighbour's. Or of the enemy down the road. Indians were afraid of Indians, Thais of Thais, Australians of Australians. When I said goodbye to people in Indonesia, their closing line was always, 'Be careful', as though they were afraid of their own land. But when you ride through as a stranger with no knowledge of the things you're meant to be afraid of, you don't notice anything wrong at all. I'm not even convinced such dangers exist; I reckon instead they're merely creations of our society's subconscious, a psychological boundary to prevent us venturing too far from home.

I wonder if that is true of all our issues and fears, that they don't *really* exist, instead they're just figments of our imagination, something we invent or exaggerate in order to keep us busy and distracted from dealing with more important things in life, like having fun. Why do we need to worry when there's nothing really to worry about? It's almost as though our problems are our clothes; we dress ourselves in them, and were we ever to take them off we would be naked, and that would be uncomfortable. But I think how nice it must be to manage without clothes for a change. Be gay, in a happy way. With not a single care or concern in the whole wide world.

Though what would we know about problems given the way people live here in India? In squalor, with rivers of sewage flowing in front of their houses. Litter piles up everywhere. There is no sanitation, people poo in the streets, ponds and rivers run green, and in the cities the air hangs heavy with smog. There is no healthcare, barely a dollar to be earned a day, and their government doesn't seem to care at all. Again, it gives you incredible respect for the people, for surviving against all odds. The worst thing is I can't see how it will ever change in India, not for the majority anyway. Wealth is centralised in the city, corruption is rife, hardly anyone pays taxes. And still we moan when we get put through to one of their call centres.

Of course, there are nice parts of India, even of Delhi. Connaught Place is one of them, a huge circular series of buildings, like a stone doughnut, built by the British and with a park in the middle. It is here that the Indian middle class park their Mercedes cars and go off browsing expensive clothes shops, bakeries and bookshops, and there's a McDonald's, a KFC and a Pizza Hut. Waiting weeks for my visas to come through, I used to go down to Connaught Place almost every day for a soft-serve cone in KFC. I'd often eat it upstairs, on the chairs, beneath the aircon and listening to MTV.

It always fascinated me, these parallel worlds created by the fast-food chains. The furniture, the food, the uniforms, the taste, the smell, the mood, the music, the atmosphere — it was the same here as it was in England. Or Australia. Or any other KFC anywhere else in the world. It's why at times like this, when I was flat, that I liked them so much. I remember arriving at the city of Mataram back in Indonesia, finding a McDonald's and sitting there eating my burger while the Lighthouse Family played *Ocean Drive* over the radio. I was seventeen again, doing my A-levels, naive about all this, naive about the world beyond my little bubble. Back then I used to stare out of windows or walk down lonely lanes wondering what else is out there; now I felt as if I knew. The world is out there. But the fast-food chains have beaten me to it.

Then it was outside, into the oven that'd melt my ice-cream if I brought it with me. I'd sometimes sit on the grass, always being bothered by men wanting to clean my ears. They had metal probes which they'd dab with cotton wool and offer to test to see how dirty my ears were. One time I let a man do it, and he fished out the biggest wad of wax. He probably had a box of it up his sleeve, or jabbed it in the ear of his dog. Though maybe my ears really were that dirty. Another man, presentable, smart, started talking to me on the way back from the bank. He said he was going back to his shop, and that he was catching a rickshaw and he could drop me off. I dropped my guard. Got in. Spent the next hour being hauled around various clothes and jewellery shops. He was on commission, being paid if I bought anything. Daft fool, me, not him. For falling for it. I told him to go away and he chased me down the street …

The same street I would later bump into Keith again, the army guy from Krabi in Thailand. That might sound surprising given the scale of the earth, but the path us travellers take is so narrow you find yourself bumping into familiar people all the time. We had a drink and he told me more stories. I realised there and then that I didn't want that — being in my fifties and still on the road. No abode, no place to call home, no one waiting for me to walk through the door and give me a hug, or even a bit of earache. It actually scared me to think that that might happen, that I might never be able to put down roots, or commit, because that's what this is really about; commitment, and the fear of it. It then troubled me to think I might always be looking for the next adventure, while the people around me are moving on, settling down, growing up, standing tall. I think this was the greatest fear of mine, that this trip wouldn't be the end, that it would be the start. And then those people would truly be gone.

It's why I always responded to those people emailing with dreams of taking off and leaving it all behind by advising that they should take no notice of me, that they should instead value and cherish what they have now, be it a home life, a house, a car, a kid, a cat, a wife, a job, a career, a canoe, a canary or a didgeridoo, whatever it is. Just cherish it. And appreciate it. Read the Sunday papers in bed, fetch a coffee from your local café, go for a drive listening to your favourite CD. Because yes, a life on the road can be triumphant, liberating, spectacular in all its freedom. I've not known freedom like it before and at times I loved it. It gave me strength, it gave me clarity. But it can also be confronting and ugly and destructive. There are sacrifices to be made in all this and often I'd wonder if it was worth it. And sometimes, often, conclude that it's not.

St Augustine once declared: 'The world is a book and those who do not travel read only one page.' I've thought about this and can see what he's saying, but what if you're already on the best page of the book, or even just a good one, and by reading the rest of it in search of something better, all you're doing is wasting time that could have been spent simply enjoying that page you're on? The counter-argument could go: 'How do you know that you're on the best page if you haven't read any of the others?' In a way I agree with that, but where does it end? When you've read all the book and you can't remember the page on which you started? Then what, pedal furiously until you find it again? Or give up, realise you've wasted your life looking for something, without ever realising it was right there under your nose all along?

No, this can't go on forever. At some point it has to stop. We all have to stop. Like I sometimes wish I could have done at times on this trip; gone back to Sydney and made amends, or called up a mate and gone over to his house for a cup of tea and a chat about old times. You meet a lot of new people on the road, but you also lose a part of the bond with those friends from the past. The world in your little bubble becomes very different to the world in theirs. The way you see things changes, your opinions, your attitudes. I knew that from the times I'd been away before. But what about this time; no doubt it'd be on a different scale. All that time on your own, that self-sufficiency and that distance you put between yourself and everyone else around you. Is that a crack you can glue or is the vase well and truly screwed? Time will tell. Tick-tock, tick-tock. I hate that clock.

I hate this heat too. I'm on the top floor of the Rooftop Hostel in Paharganj. Heat rises — it's true what they say. My room had just been painted pink, and there's an old TV in the corner and a toilet with a broken flusher. Every time I used it I'd have to fill a bucket of water from the tap and swill it down. Some days it was hell up there, so hot. The room had an air cooler — a big metal box housing a fan above a pool of water — that struggled to keep the temperature below forty. At night the pillows were drenched, the sheets too. It was sweat, sticky, horrible sweat. Three weeks of it. Iran. All because of you.

By now I'd been to see the man at the Iranian Embassy. A posh building on a nice estate; they always are. My optimism was piqued, I felt a twinge of good fortune and hope. I could feel Denise's fairies fluttering about as they made their way to have a nice word with the man on the desk. *Come on, let him through, don't make him have to find another way. He needs that visa, please don't say no, please please don't say no.* My turn. *I can feel it, I can sense it, yes, he's going to say yes.* 'Sorry, but there will be no visas for Americans, Canadians, Australians or … British,' thundered the officious man on the other side of the counter, leaving no room for debate.

The Americans and British were refused for political reasons, the Canadians for being America's neighbour, while the Australians were temporarily banned because some Indian students in Melbourne had been beaten up, in racist attacks, allegedly. What's that; the Butterfly Effect? A butterfly swings its fists in Melbourne, causing a tornado at the Iranian Embassy in Delhi. Clearly those idiots doing the bashing would have had no clue what impact their actions had, but still, if you're reading this can you please stop beating up little Asian kids? Thanks.

I rode away from the embassy feeling like one of the characters in the *Dungeons and Dragons* cartoon, desperately seeking a way out of this strange fantasy land I found myself in. Quit, turn back? No, not now. There has to be another way. Over? Under? Around? Any way round? Has to be another way around Iran. Must be. Find it. Dorothy, we must find it because no way are we flying home or turning back now. We can't do that. We will not do that. I turned to the internet and asked the world for advice. The guys on Horizons Unlimited and especially ADVRider came back quickly with suggestions.

'What about a boat from Pakistan to Egypt?' said one. 'How about you and Dorothy on a plane north to Kyrgyzstan and then across Russia,' said others. 'What about a flight straight over Pakistan and Iran from India to Turkey,' said my worried mother trying to talk me into the quickest path home. They were all ideas involving wheels off the ground or Dorothy on a boat. 'No. No. No. On the fucking land Dorothy, that's where your wheels have to stay, on dry land.' I hated looking at the map and seeing the gap between Bangkok and Kathmandu; it felt like I was cheating. I didn't want another one. That left only one option: China.

As discussed previously when looking for a way around Burma, the problem here is huge. It's as though the government doesn't want foreigners entering the country with their own vehicles in case they see things they shouldn't see, and tell the outside world. That's why they make it as expensive, time-consuming and problematic as possible in order to put people off. And it works. Few people go through China, and when they do it's usually in groups because that way the costs involved are drastically reduced.

The main burden is that you have to employ a local guide to travel with you every step of the way. I'd read that this can cost as much as US$200 a day. Someone suggested I skip all this and smuggle ourselves over the border with the aid of an unsavoury character I might happen upon in a Pakistani bar. I'll admit, that sounded quite romantic, me and Dot crawling through barbed-wire borders below the glare of Chinese searchlights, but I didn't have the confidence to try it. Even now I was still a shy traveller, keen to keep as low a profile as I could, which I think is a given for someone travelling alone, with no one to watch your back.

I contacted an agency that specialised in taking vehicles into China. David was in charge — I'd heard his name mentioned before — his agency was said to be the best. My email asked how long it would take to do the paperwork and how much would it cost to nip over the Chinese corner and get out. David emailed straight back explaining how it usually took three months to organise. I explained that my visa for Pakistan expired in just under five weeks, so really I needed to enter before that or else I would have to apply for another and after the experience, and cost, at the embassy in Bangkok I didn't fancy going through that again. He said how that was cutting it fine, but he still might be able to help.

And the price? I had to sit down for this one: US$2200 for a seven-day crossing, including guide and hotels for the night. My mouth hit the deck, my tongue unfurled across the floor and someone stood on it, making my eyes pop out. I'd heard it was a lot, but that was more than Dot had cost, a quarter the price of the original budget for the whole adventure. I couldn't afford it; by now my finances were in dire straits. The money Paul had lent me had all but run out, even the money I was owed at the beginning had been paid and spent. The trip was costing far more than I'd thought. At this stage I could not afford to ride through China.

But then came a stroke of good luck. Around this time I received an email from a publisher in Australia who wondered if I'd be interested in writing a book about the trip. They'd read an article in the *Sydney Morning Herald,* a postie bike special, that had talked about my and Dot's adventures. Now they were offering an advance on signature of the contract. It would be enough to pay my way into China and keep me on the road a little longer. A book about the trip now paying for the trip itself. How ironic. I went to email Mandy and tell her the good news, then remembered, and emailed Paul and my parents instead.

It was crazy how it all just melted together; the trouble in Iran, being told about China, David being able to get me in before my Pakistan visa ran out, the book deal to pay for it. At so many stages the whole thing threatened to implode and become improbable and now there I was, sitting in an Indian internet café, dumbstruck by it all. My whole trip had been turned on its head. I'd always thought it would go Pakistan, Iran, Turkey, then along the southern coasts of Europe: Greece, Italy, Spain, France. And now, because of the Iranians, we'd be seeing a whole different side of the world: China, Kazakhstan, Kyrgyzstan, Russia, Poland, Ukraine, Germany — a colder and much longer route, but as they say, all roads lead to the same place. I hoped this was true.

There was just one problem. To go this way would mean riding over one of the highest roads in the world, the Karakoram Highway (KKH for short), which reaches a peak of 4693 metres as it threads a path from Pakistan to China over the Himalayan mountains. At those sorts of altitudes a bike will struggle for lack of oxygen, as will its rider. The simple fact was that Dot might not have the power to climb such a height, and that really worried me because if she couldn't then I could be stranded in the north of Pakistan with a visa about to expire and no idea what to do next. To make things worse, the road sweeps up past the Swat Valley, an area where the fighting between the Pakistan army and the Taliban had been at its fiercest. This was no place to be conducting experiments. I needed to put me *and* Dot through our paces in a safer environment. Fortunately in the north of India I'd heard of just the place: Kashmir.

17

Now Climb

Indian Himalayas

The Manali to Leh Highway is the second highest road in the world and, with a maximum elevation of 5325 metres, is even higher than the KKH. It is 479 kilometres in length, takes two days to pass and is only open between June and September because of the terrible weather that affects it. It's in the very north of India, in the region of Jammu and Kashmir — the area fought over with Pakistan — and takes you between the two towns in its name. If me and Dot could manage this, then we'd ride with optimism into Pakistan. If we couldn't make it, well, we were screwed and the deposit I'd just paid David to start the process of getting me into China wasted.

In preparation, I'd posted home the aluminium box and the orange postie sacks and replaced them with a set of throw-over fabric panniers. This would lighten Dot's load and make her more agile because the weight would be carried lower down. It was also in anticipation of Pakistan where I wished to travel more discreetly. I'd also bought a foot pump and had a man in

Delhi service and wash her so now she shone as bright as I ever did see. But it wasn't to last. The 400-odd kilometres from Delhi to the start line in Manali was a mud bath. Recent rains had swamped the road, big lorries and buses had churned it to sludge. By the time we arrived in town our faces were as black as jacks.

I rested in Manali for a few days, meeting many foreigners riding around India on Royal Enfield Bullets. That was the trend. Fly to India, buy a vintage bike for a few hundred dollars and ride it around until you sell it and fly home. Hardly any of the riders wore helmets and most were on a bike for the first time. As you can imagine, there were some nasty accidents, but that's the cool confidence of youth I guess. The point of staying in Manali was to acclimatise to the altitude because already the air was making both me and Dot pant. There was a hill in the centre of town that both of us struggled up, and this was only at 1950 metres. We would be going two and a half times that. It didn't bode well, but we did what we could to enjoy Manali while we were there.

A few of us went to a waterfall just outside of town. It was a beautiful spot, the water seeming to appear from a point a mile in the sky. Then splash, a clear pool at the foot of it in which people swam. We all ignored the mad woman on the rock screaming at us and waving her arms as if to say we shouldn't be there. We thought she was just an annoyed local, sick of foreigners coming up here and ruining the view. Then *BAM*, we hear an almighty thud from above. With our feet in the water we looked up to see what the hell it was and shuddered at the sight of a tree stump as big as a skip thrashing down the mountainside right towards us. The old woman was trying to warn us they were felling trees above.

Every bounce took the stump in our direction. *BA-DUM, BA-DUM.* I was standing on the opposite side of the pool so felt fairly safe, but a group still in the water didn't know what to do. Run? Stand still? The stump could have gone anywhere, and it was bounding right towards them, tumbling faster and faster, and if it hit them they would be mashed to a pulp, flattened like the rest of the scenery it was devouring. The group split and raced off in different directions, except for one poor girl who didn't do anything; she just stood there, terrified, looking straight at it, until a second before it flattened her she bolted, tripping over a stone and falling in the water as she did so. The giant tree stump missed her by a metre; she stood white as a ghost, shaking. It was, genuinely, the closest thing I've ever seen to someone dying.

And with that we were off: the day of reckoning, Manali to Leh, a challenge that for once didn't involve a visa or bureaucracy or anything else complicated. This challenge was a simple one; to climb a mountain on a bike not designed for doing such a thing. It would perhaps be our toughest test, and the one on which most things rested. We were off to a good start; the initial climb was gentle and smooth. The road was asphalt and it wound its way up through little wooden villages, twisting in and out of their narrow streets, which really did give the sensation of being in the Alps. The shape of the valley landscape was like a giant three-dimensional 'V', fallen flat, with the road somehow climbing the point at which the two lines met.

We passed through thick forest, the gradient not too steep, it all seemed so easy; then the road turned to mud, got steeper, and everything changed. Trucks and tourist buses heading to Leh were taking it in turns to crawl up a long muddy slope, and many of them were stuck. I arced my way past and nailed the throttle, paddling desperately with my feet, Dot's back wheel slipping and sliding before catching traction and slowly rewarding us with progress, the road going on and on, up this mountain, seemingly forever, all the way to the top.

I could feel the altitude affecting her more and more. Instead of third gear I'd need second, instead of second gear I'd need first. The road now was like a skipping rope curling around and back on itself as the side of the fallen 'V' got steeper and steeper. The roadside drops were killer, with no barriers or warning. If you misjudged, you were off the end with plenty of time to reflect before you hit the ground. A truck had overrun on its way down and had its front wheels right at the edge. Men were unloading it to lighten the weight while other trucks attempted to drag it back onto the road. Another truck was on its side; it had clearly clipped a bump in the road and tipped, the margin between it coming to a rest on the road and on the cliff below not more than an inch. The drivers of those things put their lives at risk driving this road for a living.

At 3978 metres you come across the first pass, Rohtang La. It's a flat, treeless tablet of land and the first resting point after eighty kilometres of the road. A flock of tents serving snacks and tea celebrates your arrival, with no mention of the 400 or so kilometres still to go. I sat in the dirt and sank a few shots of chai, my head starting to throb, the air chill and the sky full of clouds sitting on the rugged mountains like a hat. This may have been a popular route for the trucks and the tourist buses, but it felt like a world of extremes, as though none of it was a given; that your survival of this road wasn't to be taken for granted. In a way, it reminded me of the remote homesteads in the Australian Outback and the way they would harbour a great energy that would help propel you to the next one.

Beyond that first pass the road descends along a stony, rutted causeway. Picking up speed is dangerous but also irresistible. And Dot being so light and nimble she kind of just floated and skipped across it all. I'd stand up on the foot pegs and let her back end do what it liked, weaving in and out of the ruts and bumps. It was fun and much easier than going uphill. I stopped on a hairpin corner to admire the view. As I did so a ginger-haired German stopped alongside me and stepped off his Enfield. His name was Sascha, he was only eighteen, wore no helmet and only a few weeks before had had a nasty accident involving an Indian rider who was almost killed. He was a mad bastard out here to conquer the mountain; weren't we all. He sat and smoked a spliff, telling me how after this he's off to Vietnam to visit the granddad he'd never seen before.

For the rest of the journey to Leh we rode in convoy, me and him, two lonely shadows on a mission, our engines buzzing beneath us, the wind whistling past our ears, all four eyes on the road, just riding. It was nice to have company, to ride as a pair even though it annoyed the hell out of me to keep having to stop so he could smoke another spliff. I don't know how he was managing to ride straight. He should have been all over the road. But he'd just get back on board and bomb along with his Mick Hucknall hair flapping in the breeze and his blue duffel coat billowing up. Together we squeezed past the chugging lorries and waved at the teams of workers who toiled endlessly to repair the road. There were even women and children, sitting by the roadside chiselling rocks, living in wild tents, completely filthy. They made us feel guilty for riding past, having such a good time.

Rivers ran fast across the road, sweeping off the edge of it and into the abyss below. We'd encountered a few that were shallow enough to not even bother about, but one was sinister, the water raging fast, the surface below it a rubble of rocks and no room for error or else you'd be swept off the edge. I hit it without stopping to think, just went for it, dragging my feet through the icy water for stability and keeping Dot spinning in first gear as she struggled for grip and movement while the water pounded her from the side. Water was running as high as the bottom of the petrol tank, just below the exhaust, and for a second I thought we were in trouble, but she powered on, crawling out the other side dripping. Sascha followed and as we looked back to the military truck struggling through it we figured our bikes had done quite all right.

The road got tougher. And steeper. And rougher. It was brutal, but gorgeous, an awkward contrast that made me want to stop and turn back, but also ride on to see more of it. Every so often there'd be a little village with some food stalls catering to the souls drifting by. It was a busy route, so many 4x4s and minibuses run this way, also over two days; the only other way to Leh is to fly. In these villages you could also find small hotels, though for the true experience of this road, and this wilderness, there are also temporary tent communities scattered along its length. They exist only for the few months the road is open and are operated by immigrants from Tibet and Nepal. That first day we were aiming for one halfway, giving us the same to do again the next day.

At 5 p.m. we were only just starting to climb the second pass of Baralacha La at 4892 metres. This was a killer for Dot. Every minute she'd cut out through lack of oxygen and therefore power. She would fire up again and go a little further, but then cut out again. And again. This was getting me really worried. By this stage my hands were bitterly cold. My feet were even worse, sodden from all the waterfalls and not helped by the fact I was only wearing one sock, a black one, on my left food, while my right was naked except for a battered basketball boot. I'd winged it as usual, not bothering to plan or think much of the road ahead; now the snow towered in banks along the roadside and I could feel the day losing its heat and the deep chill of night approaching. This wasn't the time to be getting another puncture, but that's exactly what I got.

I cruised to a stop on a patch of gravel just off the road. I was surrounded by snow, just short of 5000 metres. An old building with no roof and no floor was nearby. Sascha was nowhere to be seen because he was riding faster than me and was probably already a good few kilometres ahead. I got out my tools and with shivering hands and ice-block feet I set to work trying to change the inner tube. By now I'd done it almost a dozen times, but this time, whether it was my numb limbs or the disability of panic, I just couldn't do it. I couldn't get the sodding tyre off. I was panicking, beginning to plot my night in the empty building, in my tent, with no sleeping bag because the one Mandy had given me had fallen off the bike somewhere in India, so too the roll mat I'd carried all the way from East Timor. I would also have no stove, no food, only a bit of water. And it would be well below freezing. There was no one else on the road. I was alone, at the top of the Himalayas, with a puncture and only one sock.

Just as I thought all was lost I heard the sound of a motorbike. It was getting louder and I knew it could only be an Enfield, given its lazy tone. The moment Sascha burst around the corner is one of the happiest of my life. It was the sight of salvation. And of raw joy, of which I can't imagine you could ever replicate. It existed only in a moment such as this. And if we're going to believe in fairies, then this ginger-haired German was the biggest one of the lot. He'd spotted I was missing and stopped to wait. When I'd not shown up he'd come back looking for me. And found me, by the side of the road at the point of giving in. He jumped off the bike, stole the tools from my hands and began fixing the puncture while I sat staring, helpless, just shivering, so cold, so damn cold.

With the puncture finally mended and now with hands and feet like ice, we rode on, up and over the pass and then down the rotten slope on the other side. As darkness fell and our shadows disappeared, I tucked in behind the Enfield because its light was brighter. I couldn't feel my hands, my feet were numb; Dot was almost dead, and we were just lucky it was downhill so she could coast. If it had been uphill with her cutting out it would have been hell. We just kept riding, going slow, a bloody frightening time on a rutted muddy road strewn with rocks and even more of those drop-offs into the abyss. Until finally, two hours later, we saw tips of tent tops — we'd stumbled upon one of the little encampments, in the cup of this barren mountain land. We pulled off the road at 9 p.m. It must have been minus twenty. No one else was here but the hosts, three Tibetan men, huddled together in their tent with a fire roaring and drinking hot cups of sweet chai tea.

We ate a plate of food around the stove, drank steaming hot tea, and slept in one of the tents, under a dozen blankets. The bikes were outside, broken and shivering. Our bodies were inside in the same state. This was riding in the starkest wilderness and it had taken its toll. The next morning, when we finally crawled from under the covers and wrapped up as warmly as we could, we finally witnessed our surroundings by daylight. A violent palm of rocks. Raw, sinister bleakness. No mercy from nature. There was wind and there was snow. There was bitterness. There were damp gloves and shoes and a sock. I wrapped my feet in a plastic bag to keep them dry. Dot was in a worse state than any of us. She would barely start and, when I did get her going, as I tried pulling away she just stalled. She was dead, or close to it. The road had killed her.

I kept firing her into life and trying again. She'd muster just enough strength to build some momentum and from there it was simply a case of slowly coaxing her up to more than a walking pace. She was on the verge of packing up. I said as much to Sascha. I told him I was going to turn back, because to go any further would be suicide. Even if we made it to Leh I would only have to ride back along this same road again. I felt I had to preserve Dot for Pakistan, though on this evidence I wasn't sure it would be a good idea to even consider it. To all that Sascha turned around and called me 'gay'. I didn't care, call me that; I rode off in the opposite direction, towards Manali, while he went off the other way. Until five minutes later I thought, 'Bollocks to this, I'm not having a ginger-haired German calling me gay.' So I turned around and, riding like a maniac, managed to catch him up, more determined than ever that me and Dot were going to prove both him and me wrong.

That was a tough day. I was frantic for Dot. So many times she would die and come back to life. We met a couple of British bikers on Enfields who had a fiddle with Dot's carburettor and promised that would improve her — but it didn't. On some of the slopes, she would have to sit in first gear for kilometre after kilometre, the speed down to fifteen kilometres per hour. If the road took even the slightest dip, even if just down the other side of a bump, I would 'hump' her to help build that little bit of momentum, hearing the revs rise slightly. If I could get her into second gear with some revs behind her, then she would be all right. But getting those revs, that was impossible. So through this wilderness she was tortured in first gear, for hour after hour after hour. But she never gave up. Just kept screaming.

The only reprieve was a plateau that must have been thirty kilometres in length. As if God had built a table up here and smothered it with sand. It was a spectacle, like Monument Valley in America, and you almost expected to see cowboys racing through it. At times Dot touched fifty, her back end slewing through the sand. In such terrain she was far quicker than the Enfield because she was smaller than me, and that put me in charge, so I could really man-handle her. I imagine on something like a big BMW you'd be at the mercy of the machine. And be intimidated by that fact. I just kept the throttle open and only a few times considered the consequences of coming off in skateboard trousers and salmon waterproof jacket at such speed, on such a rough surface, so far from a first-aid kit because I still didn't carry one.

Then it was on to the biggest challenge of them all, the road's highest point, Taglang La, at 5325 metres. This was hell. Utter, sheer, endless hell. Dot in first, screaming in agony, my head feeling like it was going to explode for the lack of oxygen, the mud-trail road seemingly going on and on forever, a vicious drop-off to the side, trucks coming the other way. Snow beginning to fall, the wind howling, the speedo down to ten. It was endless torture for both of us. But we kept catching glimpses of the summit, knowing that if we kept pushing and riding then we would eventually make it, no matter how long it would take and however much pain it caused. Besides, we had to make that summit now. Even if we would both collapse at the top.

And there it was; the top of the world. Colin's old motorbike, bought from Joe at One Ten Motorcycles, ridden 25,000 kilometres on this adventure alone, now here, having conquered the second highest road in the world with no modifications, with me as a rider, and the weight of all my gear, standing at 5238 metres. She'd done something truly spectacular. She'd punched well above her weight. And I was genuinely, humbly, proud. Dot by now wasn't just my motorbike carrying me across the world, she was my companion, my friend; she was what stopped me from feeling so alone on this journey. Because I'd realised something: that life's a bit like a see-saw — you always need someone sitting on the other end to make it work. Mandy wasn't sitting there any more, so now when I looked up, my feet in the mud, no one to make me go up, I saw Dot, the little red motorbike with a tiny engine and four semi-automatic gears that had just climbed to the top of the world.

It was a great feeling rolling into Leh later that day, almost as though we'd survived a great disaster, though me and Sascha got separated in the traffic and I never saw the ginger-haired fairy again. As for Dot, she was in quite a state. Her front forks were weeping oil, the mad rush to change the tyre at the top of the mountain had left her rear axle threaded, her front brake cable was stretched and she even struggled to make it up the hill in the centre of town. I took her to a mechanic who told me her piston was shot and she needed a new one, which he didn't have, though I didn't believe him anyway. I tried tuning Dot myself and ended up with the carburettor in pieces and had to phone Joe, back in Australia — time zone permitting — to have him talk me through the process of putting it back together again. I was staying in a guesthouse down a back lane, in the room next to Nancy and James, a young couple touring India on a Royal Enfield. I'd been bumping into them the whole way, same with two Canadian girls, Jayme and Kirsten, who bought me a pair of warm woolly socks while I bought myself a new sleeping bag. The five of us hung out in Leh, drinking coffee, eating cake. They seemed relaxed and happy; I was massively on edge, and a curmudgeon, according to them.

Little wonder. The plan from here was to ride back down to Manali, rest a night, then enter Pakistan on the very last day my visa would allow it. From that moment on, I would have ten days to ride up the spine of the country, along the KKH, to where, on that tenth day, at the border, I would meet Abdul, my Chinese guide. I would then be in China for seven days, cutting a small corner of it, a distance perhaps of no more than 1000 kilometres. From there I would enter Kyrgyzstan, a country I'd not heard of until the detour took me that way. Here I would plan the next stage of the detour that was taking me up and over Afghanistan instead of beneath it. I calculated the detour was going to add at least 3000 kilometres to the total journey length, and in terms of time, a great deal. It'd already taken five weeks trying to arrange this alternative to Iran. Our last ride into England would be met with an autumn chill at this rate.

As for Pakistan, the country of immediate concern, I'd received an email from my cousin Jane who worked with a girl from that country. The friend had told her it really wasn't safe for me to go, and how even she, as a national, wouldn't go there herself. More bombings had been reported on the news and there'd still been no sign of the kidnapped Frenchman. In preparation I emailed my Hotmail and Facebook login codes to Paul and put him in charge of sending out the final word should it not come from me. The other guys on the postie bike, Nat and Aki, who I'd been in contact with — hoping to meet up in India but never finding mutually suitable dates — had decided not to venture beyond India. I couldn't blame them. I don't think I could have crossed into Pakistan with someone I loved on the back either. I respected them for having the courage to make that decision because I'm certain it must take more courage to stop and turn back than it does to carry on. Is it only the coward who continues to run? I wonder.

18

Bin Laden's Tent

Pakistan

Riding towards the border I didn't feel suicidal; I just felt ready. Ready for whatever was going to happen. It's not said with any intent to sound dramatic, but in the build-up to this border I'd considered the prospect of death and what that would mean and what that would feel like. Where would it take me, what would I see? Do you see blackness, for example, do you see nothing, but what does nothing look like? I just couldn't get my head around it. And I guess this is the one time on the trip I wished I'd been religious. Because if I had been, I'd have ridden towards the border with the belief that should the worst happen I would simply go to a better place and carry on, that it wouldn't be the end, just part of the process of life. But not being a religious person, all I saw *was* the end. And that scared me.

But I think it's necessary to consider such things as part of the preparation. Because you need to know that what you're about to do is worth the risk. And of that you need to be absolutely certain because I couldn't imagine anything worse than being at that border and feeling unsure of your conviction to cross it. You need to know with every bit of confidence that there is no alternative to this, that this is the only option you have and that you must take it or forever wonder why you didn't. I spent many hours thinking of the consequences and of the situations I might find myself in, of kidnap, of bomb blasts and torture, but none of them scared me as much as the thought of turning away from this challenge and flying 'home'. There was never any question or doubt about riding into Pakistan, not at any point, and I'm grateful for that or I would have struggled otherwise. It helps if you feel at the time that you have nothing left to lose.

And so Pakistan, here I go. After all the build-up, after all the fear and worry I'd generated in my mind and in my outlook. Now riding along your highway, heading to Lahore, what do you have in store? You have such a bad reputation on the TV screens around the world, why is that? What have you done to upset the people who watch our evening news? Are you like East Timor where the situation's been overblown, or is this right, you are a fiend, bombing your own, terror within, sending martyrs to blow the West to smithereens?

The first thing I saw were boys pulling wheelies on motorbikes no bigger than Dot. They were good at it, too. With their friends sitting on the back, as the front wheel touched the sky they would nod at me and I would nod back. The road was smooth and straight and all around hung the humid dust of a dry barren landscape. Brittle wooden buildings rose from the ashes, and if anything there was less litter and general clutter here than there'd been in India. Also much less colour; the world was drab in comparison, with none of the vibrant fabrics worn by the men and women on the other side of the border. The typical outfit was the salwar kameez — like a baggy pair of pyjamas — in sombre colours to match the earth.

The road continued straight. It was not far from the border to Lahore, perhaps forty kilometres. I kept my eye out, the most alert I'd ever been. Curious, nervous, worried, alive, so damn alive. Bottle this, this can be my opium. But you know, for all the worrying, this wasn't so bad. I saw Caltex petrol stations, I saw familiar fast-food names, I saw roundabouts being built and a city little different from all the others I'd encountered along the way. It had the same buzz, the same sweat, the same dreams being dreamed as anywhere else. And when I asked for directions people still took time to help me and point me in the right direction. There was no communication problem either; people's English in Pakistan was the best I'd encountered in Asia so far.

At the traffic lights I sat staring at the mass of motorcycles, their riders all in their salwar kameez, their feet in brown leather sandals, their hair neatly gelled and some with thick moustaches. None, of course, wore helmets and their bikes were all the same: Honda CD70s, the CD standing for Cash Deposit, which was written down the side as though a boast. Some had wheeled benches rigged to the back, acting as taxis. They belched out noxious smoke but moved slowly enough for me to weave between them, those new black saddle bags clearly not keeping my profile low, as I still stuck out like a sore thumb. I was just glad I hadn't covered Dot in black tape in an attempt at discretion, as I was going to, because all the bikes here were red.

I found the Regale Internet Inn down a back alley, the walls of which were strewn with posters and graffiti written in Urdu. This was the place where almost every overland traveller to Lahore stays, recommended by the Lonely Planet guide, which I didn't usually like carrying for the way you can find yourself religiously following its advice, but for Pakistan I thought its knowledge might come in handy. The man at the street café next door pointed out the entrance to the inn, an inconspicuous single door leading to a dark set of steep stairs. I climbed them, my eyes adjusting to the light and slowly focusing on the familiar world of temporary beds and pillows with occupants that change every night. I didn't mind this; in a way it was my sanctuary from the world that howled past the front door. I grabbed it with my fingertips before the storm blew me on.

Having dumped all my gear on a bed in a dark dorm room, I climbed even more steps to the rooftop, four floors up, for a view across the roaring city below. I thought I might be the only person daft enough to be here, but there were several others. Andrew and Amelia were an English couple in their thirties travelling around the world in an old Toyota Landcruiser. They too had no visa for Iran but had decided to enter Pakistan to give it one last shot at the Iranian Embassy in Islamabad. If that failed, then they were going to have to consider going up through China as well. It made me realise that I could have done that too, if only I'd had the confidence to enter Pakistan without an escape route already planned.

Daniel, another guest, was an Englishman in his twenties with a shaven head and a jovial tone. He was driving a Toyota HiLux around the world. His next destination, he said, was Afghanistan. When we told him he was mad, he simply stretched his hands behind his head, leaned back, and as casual as you please said, 'I'll be all right.' And we all shook our heads and laughed because he probably would be. He was a curious soul, though. He didn't give much away about his reasons for being out here and wanting to do such a thing. He was just here, and that was his plan, and that's all we needed to know, though I was curious to find out why he'd come up with that idea and what was pushing him to go on. Daniel wore a salwar kameez and had one outfit spare that he gave to me as disguise for the road through the perilous north.

The last person to arrive that day was Michel, a Dutch guy, in his thirties, looking much like an accountant, on a big BMW motorbike that was at least twice the size of Dot. He was also very quiet and unassuming — he was just here, in Lahore, as though he'd popped out to the shops for a pint of milk. His route had brought him down through China and over the KKH, the route I would be doing in reverse and so he talked to me about it, telling me it was fine, which was reassuring. He also excited me with talk of the countries that lay beyond, like Uzbekistan and Turkmenistan, which sounded another world entirely. I couldn't have imagined riding through such countries the day we set off; in fact I'd barely even heard of them. But then I couldn't have imagined being here in Pakistan either.

There was something very comforting about that group at the hostel in Lahore. Usually you feel a bit of a freak being the guy on the motorbike with the beard riding across the world. You feel as though you don't always belong with the other backpackers, or have much in common, which can sometimes make you feel lonely. But here, around that table, I'd found a nice place to belong, to sit and talk with people in similar situations and going through similar things, because from what I could gather we'd all been driven to the road for various reasons. We were all here with a purpose to do these things, and one day finish them. Though we did try talking Daniel out of his plan to ride through Afghanistan, but we knew it was pointless because no matter the argument nothing would ever stop him. That was what he was going to do and no way were our fears, or even his own, going to stop him going ahead with it.

And in a way that frightened me, because in him, and in me, I could see how it escalates. Almost every day you'd feel like you'd reached your limit and then something happens — you feel you have to push yourself just a little bit further, a little bit harder. It's almost as though you start your journey with the string on your kite nice and tight. You're nervous; you don't want to fly it too high. Then, every time you face a danger you're forced to let out a little more string. As the danger grows and the journey continues, you let out a little bit more string and up the kite goes, higher and higher. Every time it happens you think that's as high as your kite will fly, until the next time, when you realise you have all the string in the world. And that means one day I will probably want to ride through Afghanistan as well.

* * *

As I wound out the throttle and watched Dot's needle flicker past seventy, I kept seeing signs for Islamabad. I couldn't quite believe it; I was in Pakistan, that place I'd seen on the news so many times in the months leading up to being here. The bombings and the Taliban were apparently surging, and yet to be here you would never know it. For all the worry and the build-up, it was just another place on the map. Another bunch of people with different customs and traditions and yet the same fundamental basics of humanity — family, health, wealth and a peaceful existence — that make all corners of the world seem so familiar once you get past the visual. And so I relaxed and just cruised along, staring out to the dry bushland and construction projects just as I would have done anywhere else. I didn't ride any faster. I didn't ride with any more fear. This was just a road, and for me now the road was the most predictable, orderly place I knew.

Of course, with no more than ten days in the country there's only so many conclusions you can come to. That's what you realise about travelling; it's just a snapshot of a place, capturing a brief moment in time and space that can never be repeated. Each of our experiences is unique and it takes only the interference of different forces to swing our opinion in completely the opposite direction. Maybe the missing Frenchman had felt exactly as I did, seeing the country in a positive light, right up to the very moment he was taken away at gunpoint. It was sobering to think how easily that could happen, how easily it could have been one of us from the Lahore hostel, but I guess these are the things you have to put to one side, and get on with what you have to do, remembering that bad stuff happens everywhere, even back in England where I'd just read about some poor guy being tortured to death in his own London flat.

As for Dot, she wasn't running quite as crisply as she did the day I rode her out of Joe's shop in Caboolture, yet she gave me no reason to doubt her ability to take me to England or even over the Himalayas for the third time. She certainly didn't need a new piston as the mechanic up in Leh had thought, and as for all the other problems it was almost as though she'd cured herself. The front brake still worked despite the stretched cable, the rear axle was still held in place by the threaded bolt, the front forks still held up — despite the leak which I'd topped up — and the shoelace I'd tied around the headlight bracket to stop it rattling was holding up nicely. When Michel had told me how his bike would have to be shipped home if it suffered any serious problems, I realised more than ever that I was riding the right machine.

Islamabad, the capital, really surprised me when we arrived later that day. Given what I'd seen on the news, I imagined it to be almost in ruins, like Dili or Kathmandu. In fact, being purpose-built in the sixties, it reminded me of Milton Keynes in England or Canberra in Australia. Its streets were set out on a grid, with space made for parks and with a huge mosque at the northern end and green hills all around. Expensive German cars drove along its streets, people sat out at pavement cafés. There was a huge bookshop, and a Honda dealer. If the Taliban were coming, I certainly didn't see any evidence of panic, only the occasional military checkpoint which I imagine is normal. That said, the heavy machine gun guarding the gate of the tourist campsite came as a bit of a surprise.

I'd not seen it at first, entering the leafy yard at the invitation of the groundkeeper who sidled across the grass to greet me. Then out of the corner of my eye, I caught sight of a wall of sand bags a stone's throw away, resting on them this gun, at least 30 calibre, a soldier with his finger on the trigger and a nest of army tents behind him. I crossed the line of his sights, nodding to him as I went, and set up my tent on the acre of grass before him. It was just like any other campsite, with shade trees and a picnic table and a filthy toilet block, also used by the dozen or so soldiers stationed there. I desperately wanted to take a picture looking down the barrel of the gun, its sights set on Dot. But I daren't ask him. I wish I had.

Andrew and Amelia were also at the campsite, having driven up from Lahore that same day to take one last shot at the Iranian visa. We all wandered into Islamabad, me and Andrew in our salwar kameez, Amelia with her head and shoulders covered. We had no bother at all; in fact, when I entered the

Honda dealer enquiring about replacement parts, the owner brought me a tea, sat me down, wrote me his contact details on a piece of paper in case I found myself in trouble, and at the bottom added the line, 'I love foreigners.' He seemed genuine enough, though I did wonder if it was an obligation of faith, and not self will that had him write that. But it was charming either way.

That night Amelia cooked us all beans and bread from the back of their 4x4, which was an incredible piece of kit. On the roof was a fold-out tent with a ladder leading up to it. Inside was a fresh-water pump, a fridge and a shelving unit for their gear. On their travels they'd bought all sorts of things; rugs from India, paintings from other parts. My camping equipment was pathetic in comparison. But I didn't mind. I'd reached that point where I was happy with just petrol in the tank and some clue as to where I was going.

I didn't need much else. Just follow the road. The rest had fallen away. Even my blog and the posts for ADVrider and my website had been put on hold. In a way I was pretty naked now. I didn't have any problems, well, nothing I really worried too much about. It was no good worrying about Mandy; she was gone. Moving on. Back in Australia, a world away, nostalgia still at play. *If only … why didn't I … I should have … I could have … I must not make the same mistakes again.* But I know I will.

* * *

We were now on the KKH, which starts just north of Islamabad. We had four days to ride 800 kilometres to the border with China, where we would meet our guide, Abdul. It was a plan of military precision that just happened to have been blessed with good luck and timing, for the day my Pakistan visa expired aligned perfectly with the earliest date I could cross into China. If they hadn't aligned, it would have caused quite a hassle, and could have involved applying for another Pakistan visa. But, as things had turned out, there was no problem at all, and our only responsibility was to make sure we were there, in China, on that date.

After the Manali to Leh Highway, the KKH wasn't so daunting. I stopped in one village to ask for directions from a local man, who immediately dragged me off the bike, forced me to sit on a bench in the shade, and handed me a shot of chai in a small glass beaker. I sat there quite bewildered. I was in the middle of Pakistan, in a remote village, drinking tea with a stranger. As I was trying to explain to his friends where I'd come from, my host took a steel-toothed comb from his pocket, removed my cap and began dragging the comb through my knotted hair. It hurt like hell because my hair hadn't been cut since Sydney and not combed either. I smiled, but inside I was crying. When he was done he asked if I had any whisky. I answered no, asking him what the local policeman would say if he was caught with such a drink. 'Nothing,' he said. 'Not as long as he got a drink as well.'

Later that day, winding through the mountains, a car pulled alongside me, the window came down, a head leaned out, and in a northern accent of England a youth in the back seat enquired where I'd come from and where I was going. As we rode along, side by side, he told me he was a student at Manchester University, home visiting his family. He asked if I wanted to have dinner with them. I was hungry. Of course I did. I followed his car to a tiny village, near where the earthquake struck in 2005. I sat on the floor with his father and uncles, the women were in the building next door; I never saw them. Only he spoke English, and the food was great. He asked if I wanted to stay the night but I couldn't, I had to keep moving.

I rode a few more hours, well into the evening, and that first night on the KKH I slept instead in a place called Besham. Andrew and Amelia had driven there in their 4x4 and said it wasn't the nicest of towns. They'd felt threatened, even inside their vehicle, and advised me not to stop there. Fortunately, on the outskirts of town there was a secure government-run compound, where I arrived at around 7 p.m. With Kalashnikovs slung over their shoulders, the guards inspected my baggage, having me reluctantly reveal all my electronic equipment to the locals standing around. This unnerved me. I was then allowed to ride down the dusty drive and into the protected community, it and Besham itself, cradled in a red rock canyon.

I had the choice of two industrial-looking guesthouses, and I took the cheapest at just under ten bucks a night. The place was run by a boy no older than twelve who was quite the negotiator. He showed me to a room, which must have been his at one time, given the cartoon jungle pattern on the wallpaper and tricycle parked in the corner. It was below ground level, but up a set of steps was a little garden, with a table and chairs. The grass beneath my feet and blooming flowers were in stark contrast to the rocks all around. The sun set as I sat at the table drinking the pot of tea the boy had brought me. I felt terrible, incredibly weak because of the diarrhoea I'd not been able to fully shake off since Nepal. I was up all night, being sick as well.

I left early the next morning, riding through Besham at first light. The town marked the start of the KKH's worst section, running for a couple of hundred kilometres alongside the Swat Valley, once known as the Switzerland of Pakistan but now said to be in the hands of the Taliban. The BBC website paints the area red to signify its danger. Riding through the town, even at first light, not many folk about, I sensed this wasn't the place to linger, or break down. In fact, foreign cyclists passing this way are advised to travel by bus; those on motorcycles are usually given police escorts to ensure their safety, something most of them complain about as they argue it holds them up. The kidnapped Frenchman had apparently refused this escort.

I wasn't given one at all, being stopped at the remote checkpoints to have my passport details taken down before being allowed to ride on alone. The road was mountainous, empty and stark. And that made me wonder this: if an Englishman falls in the forest and no one is around to hear it, does he make a sound? I'll admit to being a little nervous, especially when the local kids tried to poke sticks through the front wheel as I rode past, or leapt out from behind boulders, I'm sure with the intention of frightening me into riding off the edge of the cliff. If anyone tried to kidnap me, my plan, I reasoned, was to ride straight for them, dodge some bullets and leap over the top, Steve McQueen-style. Or more likely surrender to the first shot. But I'm serious, I really did think I could escape capture if they tried.

I stopped in one village for a drink. It was one of those middle-of-nowhere places. Jagged mountains all around, sand-coloured single-room houses on one side of the road, hills running down to a river on the other. The shop was in a courtyard. I got the sense I was being watched as I entered and parked. Movement in the shadows, eyes looking on. In the shop, the owner slammed my can of cola down on his counter so hard he damn well nearly smashed it. I picked up some biscuits and he jabbed the price into a calculator with such venom that he almost broke that as well. I stood outside in the scorching sun, slugging back the fluid, tearing at the biscuits; I didn't feel welcome here. It happened at another stop a few hours later, where a couple of boys were prowling around as I drank my tea. They were squaring up for a fight. Six months ago I would have wilted in the heat. Now I stood my ground; I was ready to go. Fight, not flight.

But in a strange way, this is what I most enjoyed about the country. Whether they loved you or hated you, people weren't afraid to show it. That meant you always knew where you stood. In India and Nepal you were never sure if people were talking to you because they were friendly (or curious) or because they wanted money from you. In Pakistan I never got that impression. In fact I liked being ignored and snubbed, because it meant I could ignore and snub people in return, rather than have to act polite. I'm glad then that not everyone followed Islam's mandate to welcome all guests, especially those from a foreign land. It gave the interaction I had with people a certain authenticity. One man even refused to mend my puncture and just turned away. I respected that. And in a way didn't blame him. He had every right to hate me, given what was going on in Afghanistan, just over the border. They call the Taliban freedom fighters in this part of Pakistan. They live a tribal way of life. I'd say they have a right to that.

As for the scenery of the KKH, what is there to say other than it is a road through mountains so tall and so powerful in their explosion from the earth that you can only hope they don't come alive and smash you. There were three levels to it: at the very bottom the raging river had cut a deep trench and ploughed violently through it, the flow powered by the summer melt; above that, the plateau, green and fertile, on which the road ran, and here crops grew, people lived and the moisture from the soil would cool me as I rode through; and then straight up, almost vertically, rose these savage-looking mountains. It was staggeringly beautiful, but at all times I had to keep my eye on the road. Because up here you wouldn't want to fall from that.

19

Road Rage

China

It had been a nervous climb up and over the highest point of the KKH, the 4693-metre Khunjerab Pass. At the last town in Pakistan there was no unleaded petrol and I didn't think I would have enough fuel in the tank. A delivery was being made the next day and the owner told me to wait 'til then, but I couldn't, I had to cross into China that same day. All I could do was set off along the hundred-kilometre stretch of mountain road and hope I had enough fuel to get me to the top, at which point I could coast down the other side into China. Then, just as I was about to leave, one of the guards from the Pakistan Customs house came running out with a bottle full of petrol he'd stolen from the building's generator. It wasn't a lot but just enough to confidently power Dot to the summit.

The border is at the top of the world, with a huge stone arch to mark it. Just beyond that you get to the first Chinese checkpoint, a wooden hut, set amongst the mountains. It was incredibly cold and my head pounded from the altitude. I'd hoped Abdul, my guide, would be here, but I couldn't see him. I was instead ordered by the Chinese soldiers to dismount and take all my gear into the shed for inspection. I emptied my panniers and rucksack onto the table and watched as the guard inspected it all meticulously. I suspected they were looking for drugs, though they were even more concerned with my laptop, memory cards and camera. They took these off me, as well as my passport. One of the soldiers spoke a little English and explained that my gear would have to be inspected at the main Customs house 130 kilometres further along the KKH, or the Friendship Highway as it's known on this side of the mountain (Chinese irony at its best). There I would get them back.

I was not allowed to ride that distance alone; instead I was ordered to wait until one of the tourist buses was ready to escort me. Also waiting was a Swiss man named Sascha (a different one), about my age and a crane driver by trade. He told me he'd been hiking solo in the Pakistan mountains, going off for days on end, camping in the most desolate spots, with no form of communication or anyone to make sure he returned. His next move was to try and sneak into Tibet, which is an incredibly difficult thing to do given how strictly the Chinese control the movement of foreigners. He was a cool guy, full of spirit. In fact, on my journey along the KKH I'd met so many people just like him, including an Austrian girl travelling alone across the world on a cycle and two guys claiming to have hitch-hiked with members of the Taliban all the way out to the deadly city of Peshawar.

The soldier in possession of all my belongings jumped aboard the tourist minibus and instructed me to keep up. We were going to ride down the Friendship Highway in convoy. It was a relief to discover the road on this side of the mountain was well surfaced and in tune with the flatter landscape. Though no way could a postie bike keep up with a minibus at 4500 metres, especially not with a ferocious headwind. Our convoy swiftly developed an accordion-like motion — they'd speed off, I'd fall behind, they'd slow down, I'd catch up, they'd speed up, I'd fall behind, and so on. This infuriated the bus driver, and his Chinese and Pakistani passengers. It was late in the afternoon, they just wanted to get where they were going, not wait for the silly Westerner on his motorbike.

At one stage, the bus pulled over, allowed me to pass, and then tucked in behind me. It came within an inch of Dot's tail light, as though the driver thought its presence there was going to somehow grant us extra speed. I hated it being there, the bus filling my wing mirrors, and so I waved furiously for it to pass. Still it pushed. Still I waved. Until it eventually overtook, every face on board stuck to the side windows urging me to speed up. I looked across at them, still doing fifty, still being battered by the wind, still so very cold, still so very worn out in the middle of the Himalayas, and yelled with all my might: 'I'm going as fast as I can you fucking cunts.'

Finally, after three hours and one of the hardest, least fun rides of my life, we made it to the Customs house, a square, formal building on the outskirts of a small town called Tashkurgan. As I dismounted, the soldier from the bus approached me with a motorcycle tyre that I recognised as the one I'd bought in East Timor. It had fallen off Dot somewhere along the highway, and the bus had stopped to pick it up, something I was grateful for. I'd been carrying that tyre as a spare for months now and would have been sad to have lost it. Strange how attached you get to the things you carry. I reattached it to Dot and gathered my paperwork, ready to enter the Customs house, when a man with a clipboard approached and introduced himself as Abdul.

I was so glad to see him: a stout man, not tall, with a moustache and decent grasp of English. Poor Abdul had been waiting there all day and it was now almost 7 p.m. But for riding over a mountain pass, but for waiting two hours for the bus, but for the 130 kilometres riding behind it, I might have been there sooner. As it was, he'd had no choice but to wait because he and his paperwork colleagues were being paid $2200 to do so. I still couldn't figure out why I needed him and why China imposes such rules, especially when you can fly into the country, buy a local bike, and ride around without the need for an official guide. I met a few people who had done this. It sounded easy enough.

As for me there was a problem. Some of Dot's identity numbers didn't match those given on the forms I'd faxed through to the agency, and because the art of bureaucracy is so precise here they wouldn't release Dot, instead keeping her overnight. Which was fine, no big deal. I could handle that, sort it out in the morning while we stayed in the town that night. I just needed to retrieve all my confiscated gear. I was given my passport, then my laptop, but not the case. I asked again. I got the case back, and the new camera I'd bought to replace the old one, but not the memory cards. I asked again. I got the memory cards back. Thinking that was everything, I climbed into Abdul's car, only for one of the Customs officers to open the door and hand me the external hard-drive, which I didn't even know had been taken. What they were checking for I do not know. It would have been funny had I not been so tired and worn out.

The following morning I returned to the Customs house with Abdul. There, we learned that I was being made an example of by the Chinese Government. Our case had gone all the way to the top, not just to the local government, but the central government. I didn't get it. I was bringing my bike in for seven days to nip the corner into Kyrgyzstan. I wasn't moving here, setting up business or wishing to stay. But no, it seemed the Chinese wanted to show how welcoming they were by letting me through even though there was a glitch with the paperwork. It really was a farce, one in which I never really knew what was going on. Abdul I feared spoke in half truths and I didn't like that sense of being in the dark.

All the way from Sydney I'd been the one responsible for everything. It had just been me, dealing with the paperwork, negotiating with authorities, learning how to overcome the language barriers and all the other issues surrounding international travel. Now it was all in someone else's hands. I thought I'd like that for a change, but I didn't. I didn't like relinquishing control, relying on other people, because to them it's just a job, it doesn't matter so much. To me it was everything. Maybe I was taking it too seriously and just needed to calm down, though it was difficult, because the closer I got to England the more pressure I felt to finish this. In fact it was more worry, that I wouldn't make it. I thought about London and arriving there one day, but I never could believe it would actually happen. No chance, something must go wrong between now and then. It had to.

With Dot finally liberated, I saddled up, assuming Abdul would have to follow me; that, after all, is the reason I was paying the money. Yet he told me to 'ride ahead', and that he'd catch me up a little later as he was faster than me. I rode off, bemused, but just happy to be riding again, the road threading between more mountains, past gorgeous lakes and through canyons where a whistling wind blew. It was so cold I had to put every single item of clothing on. I stopped only for a military checkpoint where I thought I'd be in trouble for not being with Abdul. But there was no problem, they waved me through, having told me off for taking photographs, until finally, after five hours of riding and still no sign of Abdul, I stopped in a village to buy some food. An hour later Abdul caught up.

He said there was a problem with his car and that it kept breaking down on him. I struggled to hide my frustration. I'd come all this way alone, always riding at my own pace, and now I had to wait for someone else. But I didn't blame Abdul; actually I felt a strange empathy with him, as though both of us were muddling through some tricky times, so I went along with it and tried to help him fix his car every time it stopped, which was every mile. There we'd stand by the side of the road, our heads under the bonnet, both of us incompetent, pulling at leads and trying again while Dot perched on her stand behind. Finally Abdul called his mate who came out in a tractor and towed his vehicle into Kashgar.

As we crawled behind it, passing through the now flat, empty landscape, I looked down at my mismatched gloves, one still beige, one still black, then in the wing mirror at my reflection: a bundle of hair and tired, blood-shot eyes. I looked old; this journey of seven months and 27,000 kilometres had taken its toll. I had sun spots, my beard was wild, so was my hair; I had to wear a cap under my helmet to keep it out of my eyes. Dot was looking equally ragged, starting to show the effects of being ridden over the Himalayas three times, yet still plodding on with nothing more than a regular oil change and an occasional service. We must have looked quite a sight pulling into Kashgar: a tractor towing Abdul's stricken 4x4, me and Dot trailing behind.

I was going to be there four nights before being escorted to the border with Kyrgyzstan, the accommodation included in the price I'd paid for the seven-day transit through China. I would have preferred to have carried on riding, until I saw the luxury hotel I would be staying in. The Seman Hotel was set in its own grounds, a horseshoe of buildings with a garden in the middle. The room had a trouser press, satellite TV, a bathtub and an ornate ceiling, which I observed from the comfort of my bed. I soon added a few contrasting touches: my spare tyre in the corner, my dirty clothes on the chair and a litre of oil on the sink in the bathroom. I had power, I had light, I even had a woman ring me at 10 p.m. and ask if I wanted a massage; the name of the hotel seemed appropriate. I declined and had a bath instead, enjoying this period of luxury, and Kashgar itself, which was a modern, clean city, though with a very strange split to it.

In this westerly region of China is an ethnic group called the Uighurs. They have rounder, more European faces and eyes, compared to what we stereotypically think of as the Chinese (the Hans) — Abdul was a Uighur. They are mainly Muslim, and once ruled this part of the world back when it was called East Turkestan. In 1949 China claimed it for itself, sending a flood of Han people into the region and creating the source of the simmering tension that had recently flared up into violent rioting. From all accounts it was a terrible clash, with 200 dead and 1000 injured. The streets were now patrolled by the Chinese army, their trucks parked in long lines with soldiers nursing machine guns. Anyone taking a picture of the soldiers had their camera confiscated and was interviewed by the police.

This seemed a harsh country, ruled with a strong fist, overly bureaucratic and on the surface very nervous about what the outside world thought of it. Yet again, the people — those I met in the street, who would serve me kebab or lagman noodles — were just people, Han or Uighur, reacting to this stranger in the same way most other people around the world had done so: with kindness, and, of course, without violence.

This made me realise just what a privileged position you are in as an alien passing through. It is as though the world stops to put on its kindest face and greet you. Maybe the place you're visiting goes back to fighting and rioting the very moment you are gone, but in the time you are there, standing face to face, the world seems a good place, and so do its people.

Abdul dropped in every now and again on his electric motorcycle. These were strange things, with huge, white, sharp-nosed fairings and neon graphics that made them look like laser guns. They might have been props from *Back to the Future* or *Battlestar Galactica.* A lot of people had them here — you plug them into the mains and off you go.

Abdul took me to the hospital on his. It was my leg, the one I'd broken skiing into a tree ten years before. It had been a good accident: flat out down a black run, going too fast, slipped on ice, carried on sliding, unable to stop, off the side of the piste, mid-air, hit a tree, crash-landed, broken femur and pelvis, helicopter ride off the mountain, operation, bone infection, one year in a wheelchair. I'd been lucky, real lucky. In a way it was this accident that spurred me on to do things, before I lost my mobility or did it again. Now it was playing up, the fracture site swollen and sore. It was painful to walk on and I began to worry. I think it was the rough Himalayan roads that had done it.

Credit to Abdul, I only mentioned it in passing and without any encouragement he took me straight to the main city hospital. That was an experience all right, a world of total chaos, yet, like the road system in this part of the world, it just seemed to work. We queued at one counter, bought our ticket for an x-ray for ten bucks, went upstairs, wandered around the wards looking for a doctor, and finally found two of them who sat me on a bed next to a bloody pile of bandages from the last patient. When they saw the results of the x-ray they told me the fracture site was looking weak and that the three tiny metal clips that had been left in from the original surgery should be taken out in the near future before the leg broke again. The doctor advised I rest ten days before going any further. I crossed into Kyrgyzstan the following day.

20

Dogs on the Horizon

Kyrgyzstan

The Kyrgyzstan border was a desolate place. There was nothing around but rocky hills and stony bleakness. The wind was howling, the road was broken — this was the wild. I approached the soldier guarding the barrier and as I did so he clasped his fingers to form a gun and pretended to shoot me. When I stopped, I could see he was grinning, his mouth full of gold teeth, his eyes maniacal. Compared to the Chinese border post I'd just left, there were no big buildings or towering pillars of bureaucracy, only a caravan of wooden huts with a man at a window who glanced at my passport before giving it back. He didn't want to see the Carnet or even check my bike.

Had he done so he might have noticed the oil leak. It had started with an occasional drip back in Pakistan. Now it was a constant trickle, leaving a pool of black fluid wherever I left her ticking over. All of a sudden, the most dependable element in this whole damn thing, Dorothy, was in a bad way. And I panicked, irrationally. I saw this as the end. The moment it all came to a halt, still some 8000 kilometres from England. But what did I expect of Dot? She'd ridden through some incredible places, been forced up mountains she had no right to climb. She had come back from the brink, several times. Now she had three more days to ride before we made it to the Kyrgyzstan capital of Bishkek, where I hoped I could get her fixed.

Through desolate landscape we pottered, a ridge of snow-capped mountains to our left, rolling green hills to our right; the only signs of human life being the circular animal-skin tents, called yurts, housing the local nomads who lived out here in the wild. Sometimes they stood alone, other times in little clusters. Children played in the wilderness around. Horses and other animals were tethered nearby. An old Soviet 4x4 vehicle would be parked outside, and always, with absolute certainty, the family's ferocious dog would see me sauntering past and set off in chase. Their speed was incredible, and even riding flat out, pushing Dot to the limit over the wild bumpy road, leaving a trail of oil, we still struggled to escape. On one occasion my sunglasses fell off my head mid-chase, going about fifty-five kilometres per hour, the dog still snarling at my ankles, and I thought, 'No way am I stopping, the dog can have them.'

It made me wonder how the family I'd met at the border had managed. They were French, *again*, and travelling by pushbike. The two adults had a bike each, their luggage bolted to the side in huge red waterproof sacks. Attached to each of their seat posts, almost like a tandem, were the bikes ridden by their children, who were no older than five and six. They'd travelled like that all the way across Kyrgyzstan, on these terrible, winding, bumpy roads, past these vicious dogs, and were now about to do the same across China. I'd met some brave, crazy travellers on my way, but this family, they were the bravest and maddest of them all. And quite an inspiration, showing that kids and families don't have to bring about an end to adventure, though how they carried all their camping gear and clothes for the kids I'll never know.

Somewhere, between the border and Bishkek, I met a man on a horse who insisted I sit on it. It was a surreal moment; I didn't know how to get off. The man wrote his address down for me to send him a copy of the photograph I'd taken. It read something like: Hill 2, The Valley, Kyrgyzstan. Times like that I wished I'd carried a Polaroid; that way I could have given him a copy there and then. At other stops I would be handed bowls of fermented mares' milk, a sour-tasting substance with a hint of peppercorn, served in a bowl. It was disgusting, though I drank it just to be polite. I ate horse meat in one of those yurts, I even slept in a local's house after a young girl approached me as I slugged back a coffee in a lonely outpost café, enquiring if I needed 'hotel'. It turned out to be her parents' house, a crumbling white structure in the remote town of Sarry Tash. For less than ten bucks, I was given a bed of blankets on the floor in the side room and a dinner of vegetable noodles.

I don't think the parents were too keen to have me there, so while they cooked dinner I wandered around with my camera and took photos of the kids playing against a backdrop of violent nature. I left early the next morning. It was bitterly cold, with steep mountain roads to climb, some with tunnels at the top, dark and spooky. Locals in their old German cars raced through them, not seeing the little red light of the motorbike up ahead until they were almost upon us and had to swerve around. That made me clench tight. Dot continued to drop her fluid, getting worse and worse. In the little villages set amongst the jagged hills, I bought a couple of litres to top her up. I checked her level every half hour. I couldn't afford to let her run dry. That would be disaster.

When we made it to Bishkek I could have kissed the ground. Dot had survived, for now. I checked into Sabyrbek's Guesthouse, a discreet building behind a big grey metal gate, opposite the German Embassy on a leafy street in the centre of the city. It had once been the family home of a famous Kyrgyz author, and was now operated by his son as a place for passing waifs and strays to stay. Sabyrbek himself was a man of white wild hair and podgy features. In a morning he would slump at his breakfast table, flanked by strangers from all over the world. He had an older brother, in his sixties, who lived out in the garden with his wife in a shed full of junk. The pair of them were always pissed on vodka and he had a mouth that would suck up like Nana without her teeth in.

The beds were nothing more than foam mattresses on the floor, on which everyone slept elbow to elbow. There was only one bathroom, with a rusty bath tub and a trickling shower with tepid water and a toilet that was in constant use. People came and went; couples here to explore the mountains, lone travellers, others on motorbikes, like Hubert in his bright red glasses who was riding around the world for ten years on a Ural motorcycle and sidecar. His motto was 'Don't forget to take a risk today'. Another evening a young Polish couple arrived in an old Russian car with the roof cut off to make it open-top. The bodywork was painted with flowers and motifs. It was raining. They wore head scarves and cowboy boots and were going to drive until the car, or the borders, would let them drive no more. Inspiring.

Bishkek itself was a smart place, really modern and clean, with expensive shops and a surprising number of top-end German cars. A lot of money in the country comes from its gold exports. Many Russians also remain from the Soviet era. This causes some tension with the local Kyrgyz people. And the place is not without corruption. The day we rode into town, a policeman flagged me down and showed me to a fat commissioner slouched in the back of an unmarked VW Passat. He wanted money from me for being in the 'wrong lane'. I acted dumb, pretending to be a stupid tourist and not to understand what he was saying. Eventually he got bored and let me go. I felt sorry for the locals who can't use that trick.

Finally, in the gravel yard outside, I got to work on Dot. I started by removing the sprocket cover, which immediately revealed the source of the leak. It was the gasket around the drive shaft to which the sprocket is attached. It was just a circular piece of rubber. So nothing serious there, though I did find another problem. The sprocket itself was worn to within an inch of its life. Instead of the teeth being nice and thick and smooth in the way they jag in and out, this one's teeth were sharp and pointy, arching over like a breaking wave. It was fortunate, then, that I'd had this oil leak because if I hadn't, I wouldn't have known the sprocket was worn until I was standing on the spot, twisting the throttle, Dot revving, but the pair of us going nowhere. And all this way I'd never thought to check it.

There was a third problem, which revealed itself when I drained the oil. At the bottom of the engine is the bolt you unscrew to drain oil. That bolt had been in and out many times on the journey, every 1500 kilometres or so. On loosening it this time I knew something wasn't right and, trying to tighten it again, I found it just wouldn't tighten properly. On closer examination I realised the thread was ruined, so the bolt wouldn't screw tight. Since this was the bolt that held the oil in, that wasn't a good thing. Passing the blame, I thought back to the Indian mechanic in Delhi who I had paid to wash and service Dot. I'd noticed how ferociously he had swung on the spanner to tighten the bolt but had thought no more about it. I suspected this was where the damage was done. Knew I should have done it myself.

So that was three things: the sprocket, the sprocket gasket and the sump plug. And I was in Kyrgyzstan, a former Soviet state with no motorbikes on its streets, only German cars from the old Eastern bloc. Had this happened in Thailand or Indonesia there would be a mechanic on every corner, but here, asking around, there was nobody who knew a thing about bikes or where I could get the parts. Sabyrbek drove me to a local car market and with the old parts in my hand I wandered around showing them to people and asking if they had anything like it, or knew a man who did. But nothing. Sabyrbek's cousin offered to try and fix it for me, but I didn't want that. I needed to fix this myself because, dramatically, I wanted to be in charge of my own destiny, of whether we made it to England or not. If my mechanical skills failed, then it was meant to be, and I could accept it. If someone else ruined the job, I would feel forever cheated.

I had only one option: Joe, back in Caboolture. All this way, and I mean all of it, Joe had been emailing to make sure everything was all right, promising to post parts out should I need them. And I needed them now, for he was the gatekeeper to the road ahead, and I valued him as such, bashing out an email detailing the problem and getting one straight back because I'm sure he never sleeps. Immediately he began pulling all the parts he thought I'd need down from his Australian shelf, stuffing them in a box, darting down to the post office and instructing them to be sent halfway across the world to a little place in Kyrgyzstan. Without Joe's help I don't know what I would have done. The two-week delay for delivery was also perfect, as it would allow me time to make preparations for the road ahead.

My original intention was to try and drop back down into Turkey, resuming the route I would have taken had I passed through Iran. But that would be difficult. I would have to get visas for Uzbekistan and Turkmenistan, both of which required letters of introduction, which are expensive and time-consuming. Not only that but I would then have to get a ferry across the Caspian Sea, arriving in Azerbaijan, then having to pass into Armenia, then down to Turkey. There was a rumour of borders being closed, so I might have to detour via Georgia as well. As much as that was the preferred route, I just didn't have the fight for it, nor the patience, nor the money, nor the time. I needed a more direct route.

Looking at the map I saw that if I entered Kazakhstan I could ride above the Caspian Sea and eventually into Russia. West from there would bring me to Ukraine, then Poland, Germany, France, Belgium and England. I figured the distance to be around 7000 kilometres, which to my mind didn't seem very far at all. I thought if I could ride as I had in Australia and Indonesia, covering 500 kilometres a day, then I could be in London in two or three weeks. After eight months trying to get there, that was a strange thought, as though all of a sudden, after so many borders and water crossings and hurdles to make it this far, we were now looking down the barrel of a gun aimed at England. People on email reminded me I wasn't there yet, that I still had a long way to go, and therefore to be careful. I couldn't argue. But to me my home country now seemed real; in the past it had been a work of fiction, a land that didn't exist, only in folklore, and distant memory. I'd been away for so long. Now it was there, on the horizon. I had to get there before it moved again.

I got the visa for Kazakhstan with no issues. Getting into Russia would be much harder, especially on a tourist visa, as to get one you have to show evidence of accommodation booked, as well as an itinerary. I wouldn't be able to provide that, not with the way I travelled. I would have to get a transit visa instead. These limit you to just five days and require you to date your entry. That, of course, was a guessing game. I didn't know how long it would take to fix Dot or how long it would take to cross Kazakhstan. I just had to guess. And hope I got it right. The visa was issued at the embassy by a fierce Russian woman, who refused to accept my American dollar notes because they were creased. She wanted crisp ones, Lord knows why. To get them I had to give the change bureau around the corner US$120 worth of creased notes, in exchange for a crisp US$100. With that I had all the visas I'd need to reach England.

Also staying at the guesthouse were the Hülsmanns, Andreas and Claudia, a German couple riding Central Asia and Mongolia on BMWs. Andreas's bike had electrical troubles and likewise needed new parts sent from home. We spent a lot of time together; they were good company. We would set a time for breakfast and meet beneath the pagoda in the garden where we would eat bread and jam bought from the little shop next door where a girl called Nazgul worked. She was desperate to go to England to study. That was her dream. Then with the Hülsmanns I would sit for hours, making endless cups of tea, or wandering into the compact city, checking our emails, promising to visit the museum but not finding the enthusiasm to bother. We were lazy, but after so long on the road, for all three of us, the novelty of seeing something new was long gone. We preferred the familiar; that's why we sat beneath the pagoda for endless hours a day. Doing nothing, because that's all we wanted to do.

After fourteen days of waiting, the package from Joe turned up. I opened it beneath the pagoda with everyone standing around, slicing the tape with the long hunting knife I'd bought from a market stall in China to fight off the wolves. The spare parts toppled out across the table — there were almost enough to build a new bike, for Joe had not only sent everything I needed but everything he thought I *might* need as well. More inner tubes, a chain, a rear sprocket, brake cables, brake shoes, all sorts of replacement washers and gaskets, not to mention a clutch of old rags and a new set of stickers advertising One Ten Motorcycles.

Now Dot was ready to be brought back to life. Me, Andreas and Claudia went instantly to work, starting with a new front brake cable, which we thought would take us an hour to fit but in fact took almost a day. We just could not get the tension right; it either binded on or didn't work at all. The new sprocket gasket followed, which to me just didn't sit right. It moved around on the shaft, so it was back to Joe to check and yes, that was correct. Joe had also sent a new carburettor needle, simple to fit but in doing so we messed up the adjustment in the throttle cable which took an age to get right. Then the biggest job of the lot: repairing the sump plug.

At first we tried rethreading it with the tool Joe had sent me. It was like a fat drill bit that clipped into a handle. You stuck the drill bit into the ruined hole and twisted the handle, the intention being to bore a new thread. I'd not done it before and neither had Andreas or Claudia. Though shards of metal were being stripped from the bottom of Dot's engine, it was clear the new thread just wasn't biting. Andreas was keen to keep trying, but my instinct told me not to, to stop, and bodge it up instead. I wrapped the old bolt in the plumber's tape Joe had sent me. This thickened it, then with a smear of bolt glue I tightened it into a pinch. We smothered the whole lot in plastic-metal, which becomes rock hard when it dries. The bolt could not move, and to make sure, I tie-wrapped an old toothbrush up against the base so it couldn't physically fall downwards.

And with that, she was done. It had taken us almost four days, but now the three of us could stand back to admire our handiwork. Andreas's bike was fixed as well. The new ECU from Germany had impressed everyone by firing up the bike first time. After all we'd been through, sitting, waiting, sharing breakfast, getting to know each other well, we decided it only right that we leave together the next morning. I liked that: them on their BMWs, me on Dorothy, all bikes fixed and ready for the ride ahead, from here heading west, only west, first into Kazakhstan and then Russia. We wouldn't ride all that way together as they were much faster than me, but for a day we would share the road, which I had missed and was looking forward to. And things were looking better all round.

During my stay in Bishkek I'd received a phone call on Skype from Mandy, just calling to say, 'Hi, I hope you're fine.' It had been almost four months since I'd last spoken to her, back at the end of Thailand, when she'd asked me not to contact her. It had been a tough time. Every day and every kilometre I'd missed her, I'd missed her so much. I'd thought so many things, considered so many options, but never found an answer, could never get to the right words I wanted to say. So I'd obeyed and not said a thing. Now we chatted for an age, about what we'd been up to and what news each of us had missed. But it was much more than a phone call — it meant everything: redemption, atonement, the end of feeling so alone. It felt like I'd crawled out of the darkest forest, and found the sun was shining again.

21

Mind the Steppe

Kazakhstan

We rode towards the border with Kazakhstan in formation: Andreas at the front, me in the middle, Claudia bringing up the rear. At every red traffic light, Andreas's bike would stall, but it always fired back into life. It wasn't running perfectly and neither was Dot, but the fact that these bikes were running at all was the only thing that mattered now. Seven thousand kilometres, that's all. What an insignificant amount that seemed. Especially now I could just ride, with no more visas to collect or water crossings to worry about until we hit the English Channel.

The guard at the Kazakhstan border wasn't a pleasant man. He took issue with my passport for the way the ink was smudged and the pages were weathered. Blame the Thai New Year water festival in part, blame the sweat from my stomach that had slowly marinated it inside my body belt over the last eight months for the rest. Though he took issue with the Germans' passports as well, finally giving them all back in a huff and sending us to the Customs office, where one minute we needed an import form, the next we didn't, the next we did, the next we didn't. Then to the Immigration queue, where a pretty girl in front was pleading with the man at the counter to let her through. He refused point blank, before suddenly, after much persuasion, he invited her into his office, shut the blinds and I suspect enjoyed a good bit of head. She was allowed to pass through.

As were we, though not on our knees, but on our motorbikes, which now roared across the Kazakh steppe. This was a desolate place. A massive country, seemingly empty, and with endless horizons of gently rolling dry, grassy scrub. It was like being back in the Australian Outback, and once again I found myself trying to take it all in: looking up, from the top of my vision all the way to the bottom, then as far as I could to either side. What I realised in doing this was that while it was only the three of us who could see the landscape we were currently riding through, those two balls above our heads, the sun and the moon, could at some time in the day be seen by every single one of the six billion people on the planet. And that included a very special one. And when I thought of it like that, suddenly the distance between us didn't seem so very big. Look up.

Villages welcomed us every thirty to fifty kilometres or so. It's hard to avoid the stereotype, but these were just like the places depicted in *Borat*: nests of weathered homes, built on the earth and made from whatever material they could get their hands on. Were it not for the odd car parked outside you might have been in an earlier century. Then there were the petrol pumps. These were sometimes guarded by a man armed with a rifle and always you would have to pay in advance. This was troublesome as not only did you have to guess how many litres you might need but also communicate this figure to the clerk, together with the type of fuel you needed, which here went as low as 80 RON. I'd always scribble it in my notebook and hold it up to the glass window, and wait to be charged accordingly.

Then on, through the day, this convoy, travelling slowly, seventy kilometres an hour to give Dot a fighting chance. Bless the Hülsmanns for riding with me; it must have been unbearable, given that their bikes could go much faster. For me, though, it was quite enjoyable, and a surprise, because not for a minute did I think I would enjoy riding anything other than solo. Even those few hours in convoy with the BigZoners back in Indonesia had started to become tiresome, yet here, with the Hülsmanns, I enjoyed it — to have some company, to have someone to follow for a change and take the decisions and responsibility out of my hands so that I could simply sit there on my mended bike and just ride. I even left it to Andreas to choose our camping spot for that night. Though in Kazakhstan it's not so hard.

Pull off the road wherever you want, ride a kilometre or so and there in the steppe you will have the whole world to yourself. Only the moon above. We'd put up the tents on a bed of flattened grass as the sun began to set and the flame of the Germans' stove began to boil the water for a tea. Back in Bishkek I'd bought a little gas burner and a couple of bongs to fuel it. Though I had no saucepan, no cup, no cutlery, so in a sense it was useless, but after eight months on the road, I finally had my own flame. I'd even taken the opportunity in Bishkek to organise my panniers. Everything now had a place, whereas before it was all just bunged in together. My mind had always been on other things; now it had room to entertain the more simple questions, such as where do I put my dirty pants?

That night we lay in the grass eating instant noodles with bread and talking about life and motorcycles. The air was warm and for once there were no mosquitoes or anything else to bug us, only the answers to the questions we asked but couldn't quite answer. The Hülsmanns did this a lot, riding motorcycles far in the name of adventure. I sat there and thought, how nice it was for them, sharing this, being here together as a couple, wanting the same thing, wanting to go to the same places and travel by the same means. It seemed a situation too perfect to be true, but here it was, right before my very eyes.

The next morning we parted company. I headed off before they'd even got their trousers on. The expectation was for them to come shooting past me at their own pace with a toot and a wave as I dawdled along. The next time I would see them would be Germany, where we agreed that I would stop on my way past their house. They expected to arrive home a good few days ahead of me. For now I was aiming for the date I'd given for my entry to Russia. I probably had just over 2000 kilometres to get to the border and six days in which to do it. Once upon a time I would have worried about that; now I divided the days up and ploughed on, knowing that all I had to do was keep riding and if all the moons aligned just right then I'd get there, no fuss.

By this stage, I'd developed a strange sense of confidence that things would just work out — that you will get there, that the borders will open up, that things will always fall into place — simply because so far they always had. There's a famous motorcycle book called *Jupiter's Travels*, in which the author talks about a godly status that he may have generated over the course of his travels. I could never say that about myself, but you do feel a certain confidence in your ability, developed after so long of just muddling through. The best way I can describe it is Neo's bullet time in the *Matrix*; it's an awareness of everything around you, the bullets flying past, the drop-kicks coming in, the sense that you can simply side-step them, and carry on your way. It was an incredible feeling. One I imagine I'll forever be trying to recapture.

I stopped in the city of Shymkent, which rose like a mirage from the Kazakh steppe. I never failed to be amazed by just how wrong my preconceptions still were of a new place, just as they'd been of Bangkok, Pakistan and East Timor, and most other places. This city was modern, clean and sophisticated. A teenager at a bus stop directed me to an internet café in broken English, and there I sat, at a bank of computers, in the middle of Kazakhstan with a café across the road where I would later eat a decent beef burger. By now I was in email contact with Mandy, and asked if she wanted to come to England for my homecoming. I even offered to pay, though with what, I wasn't sure. But she'd got work and other things, a new life, new acquaintances, moving on. That was okay. It was just nice to be back in touch.

While in town I also looked for a saucepan for my stove, but not being able to find one, I bought a big tin of sweet corn instead. When I'd eaten the contents, it would make a perfectly good pan, as long as I held it with my gloves. I also bought tea bags, bread and instant noodles — this would be my nourishment from now on. I never did see the Hülsmanns that day. They must have passed while I was in Shymkent and would already be well on their way home to Germany. That left me once more alone. Solitude or loneliness? I guess it was more of the latter. But I knew my duty now; to just keep riding. But you show me the open road. And I'll show you another bloody puncture.

It happened as I dashed through a lazy, dusty town, fortunately right opposite a tyre shop which had a compressor and a yard for me to carry out the repair. It also had an eager attendant, quick to elbow me out of the way and show me how to do it, kneeling all over the spokes as he did so. I thought nothing of it at the time and was just glad to get back on the road. I camped that night out in the wild, alone, not even bothering with the tent. I just lay in the sleeping bag in the dirt, the knife beside me, a full moon overhead. There was always a full moon when I camped. It could have been a coincidence, though I wondered if my progress was somehow in tune with the cycle of its rotation. It had been happening the whole way, ever since that first night in Indonesia.

Perhaps the full moon was as an omen of stupidity, for the next day I forgot to check Dot's oil until it was way too late. I'd ridden 300 kilometres, full steam ahead, and then suddenly remembered I'd not examined the dipstick that day. I pulled over, removed it and cursed the air blue — there was just a faint drop on the end. Where the rest of it had gone I do not know because the sump bolt was still held secure, the plumber's tape, plastic-metal and toothbrush all doing their job. I topped it up, but the damage had been done. A few hours later I began to detect a slight unrest in Dot's engine. It happened every time I went to pull away, a faint rattle, reminiscent perhaps of the one that finished Doris 1000 kilometres into this journey. How could I have let it happen?

The next day the rattle got louder, and I grew more worried. Then, to make matters worse, the spokes in the rear wheel began to break. It was strange; everything was fine until I pulled over to take a photo of a burial monument in the middle of nowhere. A camel sauntered past. I took my photo and then went to set off again, but the wheel would not rotate. The spoke had broken while I'd been stationary, and was bent outwards, catching on the swing arm and acting like a brake. As I unscrewed the broken one and tightened up all the others, I cursed the mechanic who'd knelt on the spokes the day before. Not a single car passed. Just more camels, loping to the beat of the Kazakh steppe. An eagle soared, sand blew across the open space.

A little further along a second spoke broke, then a third. I was forty kilometres from a town. If only I could make it there.

Then a strange sight coming the other way: a cyclist, pedalling towards me. A mirage? No. He waved me down as I approached. He turned out to be a German on his way to China, covering a hundred kilometres a day. I don't remember his name, just him being there, with a little solar panel to charge his mobile phone and litres of water to charge his body. He told me a strange thing. He said there were two German motorcyclists at a café on the outskirts of the next town. They were waiting for an Englishman on a red Australia Post bike, but that this Englishman had best hurry because they'd been waiting four hours already and wouldn't wait forever.

Broken spokes, grumbling engine, I hit Dot's throttle with all my might and rode smooth and rode hard, desperate to get there before they were gone again. I didn't like being out here alone. And I'd missed their company. Thankfully I got there in time, spotting them on the steps of a café on the left-hand side of the road. I pulled up, jumped off and hugged them like I'd just won the World Cup. It'd only been two days since I saw them last, but it felt much longer, a lifetime ago. They said they were missing Dorothy too much and with no real urgency to be anywhere they thought they'd wait and make sure I got across Kazakhstan okay. Thanks to them I did.

My approach to fixing the spokes was to take three out of the front wheel and fit them in the back, my logic being that the front wheel takes less strain and therefore was more likely to cope. In confession, I was blinded by my urgency to get *there*. I just wanted to ride, not fix spokes. Fool's logic, I know. The Hülsmanns were totally against this idea and wouldn't allow me to do it, insisting instead that we scour the town on the edge of the dried-up Aral Sea for a shop that might sell spokes for an Australia Post bike. Of course we had no luck. And as we searched, more spokes broke. This was worrying. Fortunately, Claudia spoke a little Russian and was able to understand directions to the house of a man who might be able to help.

He lived down a dusty side street in a residential area. Kids taunted us as we pulled up outside his solid steel green gate and turned off our engines. They ticked in the blazing midday heat. We unsaddled, wearily, while one of the boys fetched his father, the man we were looking for, who welcomed us to his town and examined the broken spokes. He said he could help as he showed us inside. He had a huge workshop, full of machines noisily in operation. This was all in stark contrast to the town and the steppe around. Andreas handed him six spare spokes from the handful he carried for his BMW. In half an hour the man had transformed them into ones that fitted Dot perfectly. I paid him ten dollars, thanked him, and also the Hülsmanns for insisting I mend it this way, and off we rode.

These were good days, riding as a trio again, going slowly; they didn't care, we all had company, memories to share. The road was shit for miles on end, just a big wide filthy dirt track with the occasional lonely café where we stopped for goulash and tea. A policeman in one village tried to take our passports and asked us for 'souvenir'. He meant bribe. Stupidly, I was going to give him my passport to inspect, until Andreas said don't do it, just ride, and so we all took off, leaving the policeman swaying in the road, his form disappearing behind as that Kazakh steppe continued to roar — just as I did, in anger, at what I'd done to Dot's engine, which was now getting worse and worse. Andreas thought it would be fine, nothing to worry about. But I knew. I'd lived with Dot all this way; I knew when she wasn't right.

After four more days together, a short ride before the Russian border, it came time to go our separate ways again. The Hülsmanns intended to take a different route to mine, one that arced northwest across Russia, whereas I was heading directly west and into Ukraine. I thought about riding with them, given my concerns about Dot's engine; they even suggested it. But I felt that I'd come all this way on my own and it would be wrong to have them carry me the last stretch. It might sound stupid, but whether I succeeded or failed in making it to England, I wanted to be the one solely responsible. I knew if I allowed them to carry me home I wouldn't have felt like I'd done it properly. It'd be cheating, much like me not accepting the lift off the teachers, Brody and Sarah, back in the Outback.

I vividly remember the morning we parted. We were a couple of kilometres off the road, our usual encampment in the steppe. They were crossing the border that morning while I had to wait 'til the next day for my Russian visa to activate. They packed their tent away and prepared their bikes. We had one last cup of tea, then it was time to say goodbye. The three of us hugged, said, 'We'll see you soon.' Then they climbed aboard their massive bikes and fired them into life. I stood there, my tent still up, my gear still strewn across the ground, and waved as they pulled away, riding slowly across the steppe, down the trail and back onto the road. I watched them go until they were completely out of sight. I turned around and just stood on the spot. Alone in this big empty land.

A wave threatened to wash over me and leave me stranded there forever. I could feel it coming. It was one of those moments where you feel utterly incapable of doing the thing you are most required to do. But you have to do it, there is no choice, no compromise; I had to make my way home. I held my two feet firm, pushing back at that wave as it built and then slowly subsided. England was so close now. Focus on that. Focus on that single strip of road that will take me there. Ignore the engine problem, ignore Russia, Ukraine, Poland, Germany, France … focus on England. Shrink that distance, grip it in your hand. Just ride.

The next day I made haste to the border, riding for what seemed like an age before catching sight of it, a lonely outpost, like a fortress vending petrol in a Mad Max landscape. A group of wooden huts lined the approach, women standing in their doorways. A barrier was ahead of me, a queue of cars waiting, ready to pass into the compound beyond. I sat in line, anxious in the way all borders made me. You are at its mercy, powerless to the problems it might pose and only hopeful that you will be allowed quickly through, though there was never any concern that we *wouldn't* get through. Finally the barrier was raised by the guard and we passed beneath it, pulling into the compound and coming to a stop, a port-a-cabin office to my left, a bigger, stone building to my right, all around a metal fence with an opening at the far end that would take me to Russia.

I presented myself to the man at the window of the office to my left. 'You have import form?' he asked, referring to the document we were told we wouldn't need eight days ago, the day we entered Kazakhstan. I shook my head, I didn't have one. 'Problem,' he said. I made my point about being told we didn't need one. He invited me into his office to solve the dispute, the door shutting behind me. Then he pulled closed the shutters on the serving hatch. It would have been perfect darkness in there had it not been for the strip light overhead. We were joined in the room by three of his colleagues, all big strong Kazakh men, the four of them now standing over me, their arms crossed, looking down at the hairy pile of dirt, wilting in the chair. I realised in that moment I'd just walked into a nasty trap.

'You pay us 200 euros,' said one man staring me straight in the eye. A sense of unease flushed through my entire body. I trembled inside but dared not show it. Thinking back to the bribes I had paid in the past, I was about to take out the $500 I carried in my body belt; I even began recalculating my budget accordingly. I felt it inevitable, that I was going to give it to them. Then I thought, 'No, why should I give it to you, this is my money. And I don't have much. I need all this, and if I give it to you then I'll go short and have a lousy journey home.' So I shook my head and tensed my whole body because no way was I going to give up that money without a fight. The men didn't like this refusal, insisting I give the money to them; I insisted I wouldn't. This went on for a while, until finally the door opened and I was led to the building across the compound.

For two hours I was ignored by the officials sitting inside at their desks. I sat there, churning up inside. There was nothing I could do; getting irate wasn't an option either, because then I was at their mercy. I just sat forcing a smile, eating bread and dropping crumbs on their floor, blocking the door, being under everyone's feet, doing what Andreas had told me to do in such circumstances: be as big a nuisance as I could possibly be. Finally I was summoned into an office where men with honest faces demanded one hundred dollars. I refused, and they sent me back to the cabin across the yard where again I was asked for 200 euros. I said, 'No.' Then back to the main office. One hundred dollars again. I shook my head again. This went on for four hours. Still I ate my bread and made my crumbs. Still I smiled, still I waited patiently, until finally they said I could go.

I rode out across the wild no-man's land. Never had I been so glad to leave a country behind as I was Kazakhstan. I hated those men. I hated the hassle they had given me. Now I was approaching the Russian checkpoint, confident I would receive similar treatment, given the reputation the country has for corruption. But I couldn't have been more wrong. The staff there were helpful and friendly, even the stout, angry-looking woman on the Customs desk. In fact, we were getting on like a house on fire until she asked where my third-party insurance for Russia was. Surely, I suggested, I could buy it here, in

Russia, at the border. To which she replied, 'Nyet,' pointing back towards Kazakhstan, drawing a map of the compound I'd just escaped from, circling on it those damned wooden huts where the women were standing at the door. I should have bought it there, and now I couldn't enter Russia without it. There was only one thing I could do. Ride back across no-man's land and get it.

22

Hang on in There

Russia

From the moment I entered Russia, now insured, I would have just five days to ride across it and be out the other side. That meant I had to take the most direct route: from the border first to Saratov, then Borisoglebsk, Voronezh, down to Belgorod then across into Ukraine, a distance of 1320 kilometres. At any other point in the journey I would not have worried at all about this — it was an easy distance in an easy time — yet at this moment I was deeply concerned about Dot's engine. The worry was that if she broke down in those five days it would likely mean I would overstay my visa, and that, strangely, seemed like the end of the world. The pressure now was massive, just to finish, to see this through.

Another puncture wasn't the best start to the journey. It happened in the pretty city of Saratov, just over the border and built on the banks of the River Volga. I'd stopped there to get some local currency. The puncture came right beside a policeman booking people for speeding. He nodded at me and carried on. I used my last inner tube to repair it and so stopped at a tiny bike shop on the hill out of town. It was an odd place, selling tasselled leather clothing and staffed by a young woman in a very low-cut top. She had no inner tubes, so she called her dad, a man named Alex, who came over in his car and drove me across the city to a shop that did sell them. He bought me two, and gave me a Che Guevara patch to stitch to my saddle bags. Outside, while saying goodbye, two American Mormons introduced themselves. They'd been in Russia two years trying to convert the locals. Their task was harder than mine. I wished them well. And then rode on.

Things took a turn for the worse an hour out of the city. One minute we were pottering along just fine, cresting a slow rising hill, the Russian countryside all around, the next Dot had turned incredibly violent, vibrating massively and shutting down the speed to fifty-five. Trying to ride beyond that figure set her off into a rage. I couldn't figure out what had happened, though clearly it was something to do with the oil incident back in Kazakhstan. I only had myself to blame, but still panicked more than at any other time, anticipating what it would be like to break down all the way out here. What would I do? Thumb a lift with a lorry to the border? Push? Find a train? I felt worse for Dot, having come so far and now given a handicap at this late stage. She motored on, angry and slow.

I didn't ride much further that day, just far enough to leave around 900 kilometres to cover over the remaining three days. I turned off the road before a little town I could see on the horizon. There was a wood with a small clearing and I rode into that and shut her off. It was getting dark. I wondered if I should worry about wolves or bears and so I kept the knife close. I was within earshot of the road, the lorries roaring past, though they couldn't see me. I lit the stove and made tea, then noodles. It wasn't a good night's sleep; I just hoped, like you do at such times, that in the morning everything will have fixed itself and it will all seem like a bad dream. But of course it wasn't, it was real, Dot limping out of that forest campground just as badly as she'd limped in the night before, still sounding terrible, still unable to push beyond fifty-five without shaking violently.

I decided the best thing to do, given the clock ticking on my visa and the absence of motorcycle repair shops, was simply to carry on, keep her below that magic number and hope, hope to hell, that she hung in there. What didn't help were the Russian cities, such as Voronezh, where the road led straight to a busy, bustling centre. All I had for guidance was the name of the next city I was heading to. But because I'd written it down in English and all the signs were in Russian, I had no option but to try and follow the path of the sun. I asked people by the roadside for directions, but my pronunciation of the places must have been completely wrong. 'Bel-go-rod, Bee-go-rod, Bel-gov…' Blank expressions every time. I just couldn't make myself understood and rode backwards and forwards along the same stretches of road, looking for the right exit.

Finally, two old men at a petrol station pointed me in the right direction and on I went, stopping at one of the cafés along the roadside for lunch, later picking up a few groceries, and then in the evening, when the light began to dim, after fifteen hours or more on the road, I'd find a gap in the hedge and duck through it, put up my tent in the corner of a farmer's field, get the stove out, and cook whatever food I had. There's nothing better than having your bike beside you, no need to unpack it, just take what you need, set up your tent and in the morning be able to ride away within ten minutes of waking up. Remove the worry of Dot's engine and I would really have enjoyed these moments, out in the wild, eyes alert, sneaking about, moving on to another spot if I thought I'd been seen.

This being the beginning of September, it was getting very cold at night, below zero definitely. To keep warm I'd bury my head in my sleeping bag and sleep in all my clothes, feeling the cold moisture on the inside of the tent. I even opened the survival blanket Claudia had given me and wrapped myself in that like a Christmas turkey. With no roll mat I could feel every rut and bump in the ground. With only two tent pegs left, I used a screwdriver and a spanner to keep the other ends down. Sometimes I'd light the stove inside the tent just to warm it up.

If my battery would allow it, I would open up the laptop around 9 p.m. — bedtime wasn't long after — and play a few songs as I lay back and reflected on the day, thinking about the past and the future and the bits in between. Mandy was in that tent with me. Always at the handlebars as well. An Australian guy in Bishkek had given me a Bernard Fanning album and I liked that. It really suited my mood, listening to songs that pick you up and brush you down and give you a stern talking to and give you the strength to scream 'COME ON' just one more time. This focused my mind for the night in the tent by that Russian road, in the freezing cold, buried in my sleeping bag and smelling badly, having not washed or even changed my underpants in the ten days I'd been riding since Bishkek. No wonder Mandy didn't want to come to my homecoming.

Then the morning would come and I would rise with the sun, crawling out of the tent, colder than ever, shivering, firing up the stove and boiling some water in my sweet-corn tin. I had no milk or sugar, but I had a tea bag and that was enough. If I had bread, I'd dip some in the tea. The ground around me would be covered in dew. I would survey the scenery, maybe do a crap in the hedge, then I would begin to pack, rolling up my tent and sleeping bag, strapping it all to the back of Dot who'd had the key left in her all night just so I didn't lose it. I would scour the ground to make sure I had everything, put on my helmet and gloves — now with socks over the ends for extra warmth — and then I would sit on Dot, and hope she was going to start.

This was now always a tense moment — turning the key and watching the light go green, pulling out the kick start, pausing, injecting her cylinder with positive thoughts, then stroking downwards with my right leg. Of course she started. Of course she carried me out of that field and back onto the main road, which we now followed in a southwesterly direction, still doing fifty-five, still counting every kilometre, worrying each and every single one. It was a long, slow slog across Russia in those five days, with all my hopes pinned on reaching the Ukraine border. Twenty kilometres from it, Dot had another blip, this time down to forty kilometres an hour, my heart in my mouth, easing off the throttle until she gathered herself again. She continued on.

The Ukraine border was another nasty experience. It started okay, the process of leaving Russia pretty painless except for the minibus of young football players who goaded me. I fingered the Chinese hunting knife stored in the bag strapped across Dot's tank — the bag a gift from James back in India — and felt like showing them my mood. But I didn't, I waited in turn, and, when allowed, went through, stopping at the duty-free shop in no-man's land to buy a dozen packets of cigarettes because I'd heard they were handy for bribing the merciless Ukrainian police. At the Ukraine border itself, there was a discrepancy over my Carnet, the guy on the Immigration counter tearing a strip out of his colleagues further along at the Customs house. Having been on the receiving end of this outburst, the Customs officers took out their frustrations on me.

One man, a shifty-eyed, evil-smirking son of a bitch, directed me over to a corner well away from anyone else. I sensed trouble in an instant, my instinct and judgement now well honed to these things. And sure enough, over the next three hours I was made to empty out all my belongings and scatter them across the floor for the man to examine and probe in great detail. A sniffer dog was then brought around, the sight of which filled me with dread, even though I had nothing to hide. They checked inside my wallet and my boots, became suspicious over the water-purifying tablets I'd bought in Nepal, and for a minute even thought a spare One Ten Motorcycles sticker was one big LSD tab. The man liked my Chinese knife, wanting to use it to loosen the screws on the back of my laptop to check for drugs or anything else he thought might be hiding in there.

I'd brought that laptop all the way from Sydney. Somehow it had survived the distance, being rattled about in the aluminium box, getting wet, being dropped in Bangkok and needing a new power socket. I treasured that laptop as much as I treasured everything else I'd carried so far — even the clothes I'd abandoned along the way had had their sleeves ripped off and tied around the handlebars as reminders of the part they had played. The worn-out sprocket was tied there as well. And no way was that laptop going to be ruined by this guy, so I stiffened up and told him, 'No', quite ferociously. Strangely he obeyed, turning his attention next to Dot, examining her just as thoroughly. I had to remove the seat so they could check inside the petrol tank beneath, then the headlight cover, and the side panels, and behind the battery. I shook like a leaf throughout. My hands trembling. The guard noticed that. I tried my best to tame them.

At one point a man drove through the border in his car. We made eye contact. He could see my anguish, and so in Ukrainian asked the guard why I was being treated like this. The guard answered him and in broken English the man relayed to me that it was because I had been through Pakistan and therefore under suspicion of carrying drugs. I could see how that might work: ride a bike from Australia to Pakistan, pick up some gear, then ride the rest of the way across the world to deliver it to England. As odd as that suggestion was, I just had the most awful feeling that any moment now they were going to produce some mysterious substance and allege it was mine. When one of the guards gave me a 'souvenir' key ring I threw it into the gutter as soon as he wasn't looking. I feared it to be a set-up. Finally, with all my gear scattered across the floor, Dot in pieces, the Customs officer said, 'Pack up', and walked off.

It was a rough night at my camping spot just over the border. A missing tent pole meant the whole thing had collapsed so I wrapped myself in the fabric like a human fajita and buried myself deep within the undergrowth as the rain fell. My matches were wet, so I had no heat, no tea, no food other than bread. My trousers were falling apart, Dot's panniers were ripped, I'd not showered or changed my clothes for thirteen days, my eyes were red and we still had another 2000 kilometres to go. Home never seemed as far away as it did that night buried like a Mexican dish in the Ukrainian hedge. Did I want to be there, in England? In one sense I did — I wanted to see if me and Dot could make it — but did I actually *want* to be in England and not live this life any more? That's much tougher. This was who I was now, content with this existence. I wasn't quite sitting on a park bench waiting to be fed. But I could see the similarities.

On the outskirts of Kiev the following day, I stopped at the golden arches to check my emails. I did this every time I saw

8,000 KILOMETRES (APPROX)
RUSSIA
5 DAYS
ENGLAND
1 DAY
GERMANY
7 DAYS
POLAND
3 DAYS
SEARCHED FOR DRUGS
ASKED FOR 200 EUROS HERE
UKRAINE
5 DAYS
KAZAKHSTAN
10 DAYS
FRANCE
BLACK SEA
CASPIAN SEA
TURKEY
IRAN

one now, dashing inside and ordering a burger before sitting down and firing up the Hotmail, just in case. You never know, just maybe she'd changed her mind and decided to come. Not today. There was an email from my dad though. He'd read of my engine troubles and was on standby to drive all the way out from England, to Ukraine, with the engine out of the Honda C90 I bought to do the trip the first time around. It was still in the shed. Dad was convinced the engine would bolt straight into Dot and so told me to just let him know and he would bring it out to wherever I was. I was so proud of him for suggesting this. And in a way I hoped it would happen, just so he could stretch his own legs.

And so very nearly it did. We were on the final approach to the Polish border, the time around 5 a.m. and the bitterly cold mist rising up from the marshland by the roadside. The speed was still fifty-five and I knew if I carried on like this we'd be in Poland in a couple of hours having crossed Ukraine in just four days. Dot seemed fine, but then she went into meltdown. It was like someone had pushed her off-switch; she simply died. And in that split second I thought that was it. I patted her tank and congratulated her for bringing me this far. I promised to get her back safely, either by train or, if necessary, by pushing her. In fact I thought it only fair that she finish this under my own steam, calculating it would take a hundred days to push her to England from here.

But I should have known better than to rule out this little postie bike. Someone once told me you can't kill one, and they were right, because, on the very brink of death, when I thought it was all over, very slowly, very gradually, she came back to life. Hovering around ten kilometres an hour, then slowly rising, more and more response in her throttle, which ever so slowly I began to open, coaxing her, talking to her, willing her on. The *Forrest Gump* music played as she broke from the leg irons and began to run. I'm sure it's possible to attribute this to her engine temporarily seizing and then releasing as it cooled down, but to me this was a resurrection. This was Dot saying, 'No, this isn't going to finish here, I'm not going to be pushed over that finish line, I'm going to make it myself.' And with that she ran, and she ran.

Back up to speed, twenty … thirty … forty … fifty … fifty-five … hold it there, just keep holding it there. We were now seventy kilometres from the border, and still the mist swirled, still every part of me was freezing cold and shivering, still we were only in Ukraine with such a long way to go, but hell, to me this was a signal that however bad it got, however much she struggled on this final stretch, she was going to make it, she was going to carry me home. And the realisation of that was liberating, freeing me from the worry and giving me even more respect for this machine that had been buzzing between my legs for the last 32,000 kilometres, barely skipping a beat. We reached the Polish border and after another saga with Customs officials who didn't believe where I'd come from, we were through, to Poland, the start of the EU.

23

Final Stride

Poland

My intention was to carry on camping all the way through to England, but on the road just north of Pryzemśl, Poland, I spotted a motel and thought, why not; after all, I'd not had a wash or a change of clothes since Bishkek, now 5000 kilometres ago. I must have looked a complete state checking in, the girl on the desk staring at me in bemusement. *Who was I, where had I come from, where was I going?* I dumped all my gear in the room and stripped off my clothes, amazed to see skin and a body still there, though now I was slimmer, and paler, and my eyes ached from the road they'd been tracing for so long. It was gorgeous to have a shower, to just stand there and let the water fall down, trying to untangle my hair and finding it impossible for all the knots. It hadn't been combed since the man in Pakistan had just about ripped it out with his metal comb.

That night I ate pepperoni pizza and even had a beer. I was enjoying the moment. It was incomprehensible in a way. I just could not compute that in the last eight and a half months the road had brought me from Sydney to here, through East Timor, Indonesia, Malaysia, Thailand, Nepal, India, Pakistan, China, Kyrgyzstan, Kazakhstan, Russia, Ukraine and now Poland, with just Germany, France and maybe Belgium to go. That distance felt tiny, just a speck on a map, one of which I finally bought for Europe and realised Germany wasn't where I thought it was, a little more to the north and to the east than I'd expected — the last big country to cross. But first Poland, one of the prettiest places I'd been through.

It was green and blue, the sky and endless rolling countryside all around. Yet it was modern, and perfect in the way it straddled the fence between the two extremes that brought us the Berlin Wall. There was that sense of unity, of brotherhood about it, yet it was as modern as England; I could drink the water from the tap and pay for my petrol by debit card. I even came across an official Honda dealer for the first time since Pakistan and despite Dot giving me no reason to believe she wouldn't make it now, I braked from fifty-five and steered her in, coming to a halt in the yard and asking the mechanics if they'd take a look.

A young mechanic named Bartek began the process of checking her over. By chance he had once worked in the bacon factory not far from where my parents live in England. He said he liked the old people of England but thought the young ones were rude and violent. That was good. It sounded like nothing had changed in the time I'd been away. About Dot he said there wasn't too much wrong. The valve clearance was too tight, and he cleaned the carburettor and did a compression test, but other than that he could only attribute her current state to old age. She was simply worn out. We changed oil while we were there, having to suck the old fluid out with a syringe because, with the sump bolt glued into place, she wasn't able to be drained the usual way. It was testament, though, to mine and Andreas's bodge job that the bolt had stayed in. Even the toothbrush was still there.

Across the rest of Poland ran a motorway, three lanes, with vehicles travelling incredibly fast. This wasn't the place for a bike going so slowly, but I wasn't taking the back roads now, I was too keen to reach dry land. And I tried, through the night, dodging trucks as I tucked in tight to the hard shoulder until I realised if I went much further I was not going to survive the night. A truck driver would feel a little ripple, thinking it of no significance, as me and Dot were squashed beneath his wheels. I pulled into a truck stop around midnight; it was drizzling and there was nowhere for me to sleep. The ground was gravel and with a tent pole still missing it was no good even trying to put the tent up. Instead I lay myself across Dot's seat, my feet over the handlebars, my head back on the rear brake light, in my sleeping bag, with the fabric of the tent pulled over me to keep the rain off.

Inadvertently, I'd placed myself in the corner where all the truckers came for a wee. As I tried to drift off all I could hear were the footsteps of another man crunching across the gravel, unzipping his fly before proceeding to water the ground only half a metre from my ear. I thought about getting up and moving but I couldn't be bothered; I stayed where I was and drifted in and out of sleep, changing positions, trying not to tip over as I did so because inside my sleeping bag I still had my Chinese hunting knife, just in case those wolves came. I couldn't wait for the sun to come up; then I could get back on the road. My plan was to cross Poland in no more than four days, and nothing was going to stop me from doing that.

By midday we had passed Warsaw. The sky was angry and menacing as I did so, the black clouds suggesting my salmon pink overalls were about to get wet. Then a moment, one I shall always remember, when a hole in the clouds opened up and a bright ray of sunlight shone down. I stared at it until, after a few seconds, the clouds moved on and it was gone. Had I been a religious person I would have seen that as a sign from God that I was almost home, but I still didn't believe in being carried across the sand by a divine force, so I just appreciated the beauty of the moment. Actually, I wasn't sure what I believed any more. Maybe not in God, as a person, but in something. I had to, having made it all this way with no serious injury or incident. Fairies, angels, the Soul of the Earth as it's called in the book *The Alchemist*; who knows? But I believed in something, even if it was just that everything works out in the end.

In Dresden, the first German city I came to, I wandered around in a daze, watching the tourists take pictures of the rebuilt cathedral the RAF had flattened in the war, Dot parked on the cobbled streets as the trams came past and the clock tower chimed. I ate a hot dog, watched the punks and skaters in the park, then wandered into a camping shop and got excited about all the gear I'd never bought and never actually needed. I even thought about getting a tattoo in one of the parlours, though I couldn't decide on the design. Someone suggested I should get a single small black circle, a Dot. I even enquired as to how much it might cost and it wasn't a lot. But I chickened out.

I carried on, walking through a shopping centre, looking for a place to change some money. I spotted a woman with a pram. She was Muslim, wearing a heavy black veil covering everything but her eyes. I recognised her from Indonesia, from India and from Pakistan, and I felt great empathy towards her. I knew what it was like to be the odd one out, a stranger in a foreign land where people watch you with suspicion, not sure whether to trust you, pointing you out in the street, laughing and thinking deep down that you should clear off and go home. She might have been frightened, apprehensive, just like I had been in East Timor and elsewhere. To come from Pakistan (or wherever it was) to here must have involved a terrible culture shock. Nervous and brave; that's how I pictured her beneath the veil.

A strange thing happened the day I rode out of Dresden. I was filling up Dot at a station when a car pulled up behind me. The driver and passenger got out and walked towards me. 'You don't recognise us do you?' said the man as he stuck out his hand.

'No, sorry I don't.'

The man explained: 'You remember, Khao Sok National Park?'

'Yes,' I said.

'And the leeches,' he added.

Oh yes! It was the German couple I'd walked with along the trail and then said goodbye to at the end, not thinking much of it as I certainly didn't expect to see them again. Yet, here they were, five months later, at a petrol station just outside Dresden. They'd spotted Dot and thought, it can't be. But it was. And it was great to see them again, even if I didn't remember their names or know a single thing about them.

I rode the autobahns across Germany. These have no upper speed limits, and cars would come roaring past at more than 200 kilometres per hour. But they do have lower speed restrictions — sixty kilometres per hour — which Dot wasn't quite able to reach. The police pulled me over three times for being too slow. Of course as the blue flashing lights came screaming up from behind I'd hit the accelerator extra hard to try and nudge her speed up, and when they questioned me on such things I'd pretend we'd been doing well above sixty all along. It always took a while for them to believe where we'd come from, and I'd have to produce all my documents to satisfy them, at which point they'd send us on our way with a handshake. The passing motorcyclists weren't so impressed. If I waved, they never waved back. And when I stopped to help a stricken Harley-Davidson, the guy just blanked me. Fine.

The Hülsmanns were much more pleased to see me. It had been almost two weeks since they'd left me on the Kazakh steppe, and they'd been home three days before I dropped by. With time to spare before the day I was due to arrive in Dover,

I hung out with them for a few days, driving to a town just outside Cologne for some sausage and curry, using their internet to book my ferry ticket, and sitting to watch the Ewan and Charley shows. That was fascinating. To see how they did it, obviously in a very different way, though I'd say with equal difficulty. To have gone through that with a camera in your face at times must have been tough. When you're at your lowest, you just want to sit and think, listen and breathe, but instead they had to smile and perform for the camera.

I wondered, though, if I'd watched Ewan and Charley properly, back in Sydney, would I still have set off? I doubt it. I think I would have considered it beyond me. That's why it was now so interesting to watch. To see the equipment and the training and the planning they put into it, though in some ways I had the only planning you really need — to be certain that it's something you *have* to do. Not want to do, because that's not enough. I think there's got to be the understanding that there is no other way out; this is your only option, and therefore you *must* do this or forever wonder, what if? It was this that prevented me from ever quitting, or turning back, despite at times the incredible urge to do so. My advice for anyone wanting to ride across the world on a bike is to look around, see what you're going to risk, then ask yourself if it's worth it. Because once you've gone, you've gone. Though Sven on the pushbike had gone back for Caroline — for love.

I left the Hülsmanns, our third goodbye, the handshakes now stiffer, the hugs even longer. Instead of heading straight for the French coast, I took the opportunity to drop south, almost following the border as I worked my way through the German countryside, some of the best scenery I'd seen, with cute little hamlets sitting deep in the valleys. Little red Dot screamed along the winding valley roads, still doing fifty-five, her rider still looking up at the sky and down at his welding gloves and old boots, still intact after all this time. My big white helmet had also survived and Kevin Rudd's signature, while faded, was still there. He'd ridden the whole way, even though he daren't come to Bangkok.

To look at, you'd say none of this equipment was really up to the job, and yet it had survived, most notably the salmon pink suit given to me by the man in Nepal. I was so grateful for it now — it kept out the wind and the cold — and the ingrained dirt was beginning to take the edge off the colour. Though sadly, this clothing wasn't sufficient, apparently, for the Nürburgring, a famous German racetrack open to the public for a small fee. I was going to take Dot around for a quick lap, heading there especially, but the marshal didn't like the look of my skateboard trousers, or the hint of our top speed. And so wouldn't let us on. The Porsches, I could see, were scared. I camped there that night. Then woke the next morning; this was it, after 258 days, the last one on the road.

I was going to make it count by detouring through Luxembourg and Holland in order to bring my country tally up from eighteen to twenty, but in the end I couldn't be arsed, so I took the most direct route, into Belgium and along the main highway towards Brussels. On the approach to the city, in towns and villages, there was a surreal scene: young hot women in the shop windows wearing virtually nothing but an expression that said, come in and pay me for something special. Next door would be the newsagent or the baker. This was in the middle of the day, and of all the things I'd seen and encountered on my journey across the world, this was perhaps the oddest of them all, and in Belgium of all places. I settled for an iced bun and rode on.

The road through Belgium that evening seemed to go on and on forever. I kept checking the map and making a note of the distance markers, which barely seemed to move. It made me wonder all of a sudden how I'd done so many endless hours on the road, never really finding the kilometres a struggle, until now. Strangely, I'd never been bored riding, often amusing myself in song or in thought, and always looking at the world around me and the people whose eyes I was still making contact with in every village along the way. I must by now have met a million. But no more now, as darkness had fallen; the roads fell quiet, only the buzzing noise of a small engine slowly propelling me through the jet black night.

We hit the French coast around midnight. It was freezing cold, the mist swirling and no one else on the road. I wore all my clothes, gloves and socks on my hand. This was it, not just the final day, but the final stretch. I traced the road, alongside a water ditch. I kept my eye out for illegal immigrants as there'd been reports of people being robbed by them. I spotted one in the mirror. He had a bushy beard and tired eyes. I thought of the journey now, from Sydney to here. It wasn't regrets, just acceptance. Of everything: me, her, the way we were, the way things turn out, often without intention or conscious thought. But not by accident either. Nothing, really, can be put down to fate, or chance, as I might previously have thought. It's down to us. The good things, and the bad. The buck stops here. And so does France.

It was 2 a.m. when I entered Calais and followed signs to the ferry port. The town was empty — dark urban streets leading out to the sea. True to form, this couldn't all end without one last little hitch, which I discovered in the ferry company's booking office when I went in to confirm my ticket. 'Your ferry sailed three days ago,' said the man at the desk. Damn it, I'd booked the wrong date. There was nothing I could do but buy another ticket for the ferry leaving six hours later, the one I'd intended to be booked on. With that I walked out beneath the floodlights, picked my spot in the carpark and went to sleep on the ground. This would be the last time I wrapped myself in the tent, the last night I would sleep in the shadow of Dot, the last night I would wake up and have to ride the next morning.

It was an odd sensation on the ferry that morning. I was neither happy nor sad at this moment; I was numb, overwhelmed and underwhelmed. An anti-climax in that sense. The fact that my friends and family would be waiting at the other end didn't seem at all real. How could they be there? I'd not seen them for eighteen months; surely they won't be in the same place as me, that can't be possible. Then over the loudspeaker came an announcement: on board was a chap who'd just ridden his 105cc Australia Post bike all the way from Sydney. I later found out that Paul, the good friend who'd lent me money back in Malaysia, had alerted the ferry company. As a result I was offered a glass of champagne and a free cooked breakfast. I took a coffee instead of the champagne.

As I sat and drank it, a trickle of people came over to congratulate me. How did they know it was me? Maybe it was the hair and the beard and the clothes that had survived nine months on the road. Maybe it was the BigZoner jacket I'd worn all the way from Indonesia. I told these enquirers about my adventure as though I was talking about someone else, because I wasn't convinced I was the one who'd done it. Nine months ago I was working in a café in Sydney making sandwiches for business people at lunchtime. From there to here, leaving after only two days, saying goodbye on the doorstep, nothing to do but run, take to the road and see how far I could follow it. It wasn't a sense of pride or excitement I now sat and nursed, just relief. I was glad it was all over.

And with that, the ferry docked. Me and Colin's old motorbike had made it to England.

24

Home

Dover, England

Mum flung her arms around me and squeezed what life was left in me completely out. I could excuse her given what I must have put her through the last nine months. My dad approached in his usual loping manner and said, just as I'd imagined he would, 'So you made it then?' Aunty Pat and Uncle John were there, so too cousin Jane, the one with a friend from Pakistan, and her husband Grant. Sadly my nan couldn't make it, not well. Then I noticed on the other side of the carpark, hidden by the pillars of the flyover bridge, another crowd, of at least twenty, maybe more, holding banners with 'Welcome Home Big Teeth' in big painted red letters. It was my friends from school, from uni, from various internet forums who'd caught wind of my arrival and come down to have their picture taken with Dot, and warm her seat with their bottoms.

A pair of police officers stood guard, thinking we were protestors, but they didn't seem in any rush to move us on. It was quite a baffling moment, faces and hands coming at me;

where's my knife, do I fight them off? No, shake their hands, and give them a hug and thank them for coming and for their support along the way because I'd certainly needed it. I'd not been as alone as I'd thought on the road, as much as it sometimes felt, or I wanted to believe. I felt a bit of a fraud in a way; they'd been privy only to one version of the truth, the one I'd presented in my group emails, which gave only one side of the story. There were others; this one, that one, Mandy's. All the same, but different.

Finally we made a break for the McDonald's at the top of Dover Hill, the white cliffs somewhere off to the right. It seemed like a fitting meeting place given how the fast-food chain had kept me in sustenance and free wi-fi all the way from Russia. We didn't linger long as we still had to reach the unofficial finish line in London. Paul led the way in a white Mercedes van that Dot sat behind, gradually taking advantage of the slipstream. With no fears over breaking down, I opened up the stops, blasted past the fifty-five limit I'd been sticking to for the last 6000 kilometres or so and watched as the needle twitched past sixty, then sixty-five, then seventy, until she was stuck on seventy-five and didn't seem at all fussed. Well I'll be darned. I could have been home the week before if only I'd known. Though it was probably because I'd treated her so gently that I could be rough with her now. And now she liked it, dirty wench.

The countryside of England was a real pleasure to ride through, still so green and blooming despite it being late September. I liked the thick hedgerows and the church spires, the old pubs, and the signposts that for once I could read. I liked the look of the people and the smell in the air. Suddenly England seemed unique. Home? I'm not sure. It was too early to tell. It was just so weird, looking in my mirror and seeing my mum and dad's faces in the front seats of the Volvo behind me. What were they doing there, how had that happened? It was a happy moment, to have made it, to have finally finished the journey, taking just under nine months, covering 35,000 kilometres, riding through eighteen countries and costing … I haven't a clue. More than $8000, that's for sure.

It was a beautiful afternoon in London as the convoy made its way through the outskirts. The sun was shining and the pavements were full of people enjoying the warm weather. I'd never really appreciated just what a great city it is, not until this moment when it all seemed so novel. It was the architecture, and the pace of it, the red buses, the black cabs, even, dare I say it, the multiculturalism. Pretty much every place I'd passed through on my way had been populated by a certain race, ethnicity. Now here, there was everyone. The faces I'd seen in Indonesia, in Thailand, in India, Pakistan, Kazakhstan, Russia, were now all together, queuing at the bus stop, playing in the same park.

Our destination was the Ace Café, a famous biker hangout on the northwest side of the city. People with Harley-Davidsons and Ducatis tend to go there, proper bikes, though I doubt it had received anything more proper than a 105cc Australia Post bike that had ridden across the world with barely any issues, certainly in spite of my stewardship, not because of it. Dot took her place on the stage, most of the people in the bar wondering what such a crap little bike was doing there, but she looked impressive that day, caked in dirt and weighed down by all the saddle bags. The toothbrush still holding the sump plug in, the shoelace still holding her headlight on, the old sprocket still tied around the handlebars, the BigZoner bell still chiming, the plaque still bolted to the back. Colin's old motorbike had not only carried him across the Outback but also this whingeing Pom across the world. With that I had a pint and a plate of chips and took one almighty sigh. The journey was over.

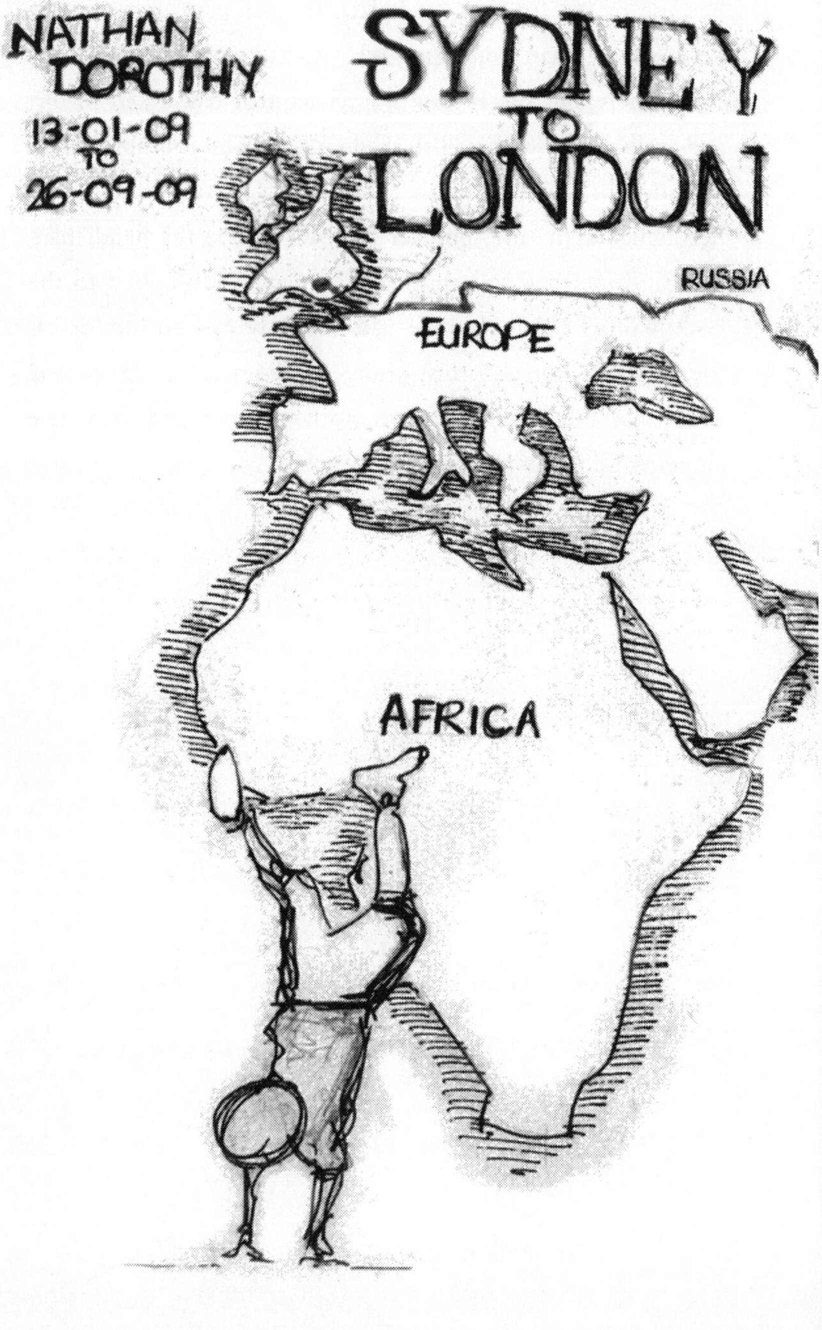
NATHAN DOROTHY
13-01-09
TO
26-09-09
SYDNEY
TO
LONDON
RUSSIA
EUROPE
AFRICA

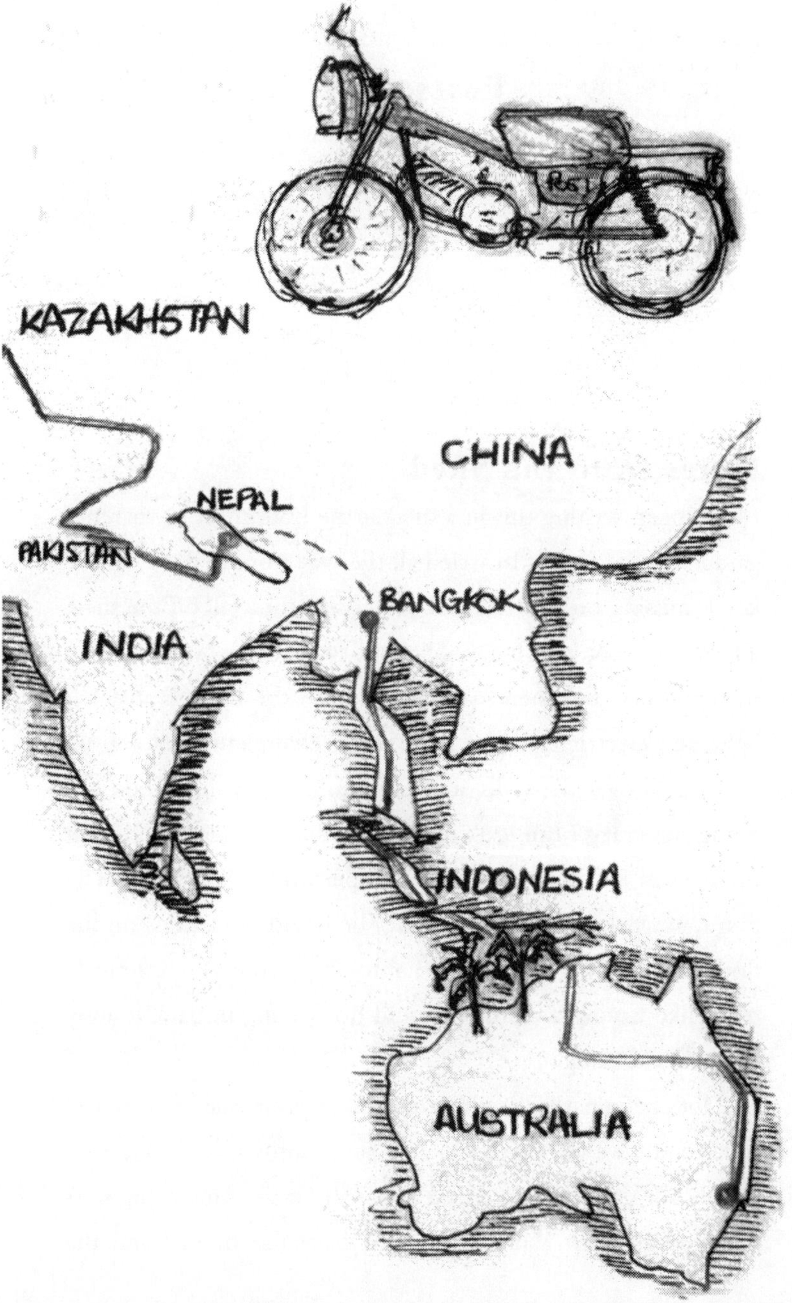
KAZAKHSTAN
CHINA
NEPAL
PAKISTAN
BANGKOK
INDIA
INDONESIA
AUSTRALIA

Postscript

Notes from the Shed

I have been writing this in a shed at the bottom of my parents' garden on the laptop I carried all the way from Sydney. The 'u' key is missing on it after a can of Russian tuna fell off the shelf. The shed is not very big, only about two metres by three, with no windows, and there's a draught from the door. But it has light and electricity, and a desk and a chair, and photos from my trip all over the walls, just as a reminder, so that when I'm going stir-crazy I can look up and see that there is a world out there, even if I don't recognise the person in the picture. The first few weeks I even slept in the shed, with a mattress on the floor. Gradually I have moved into the house and I actually quite like having a comfy bed and not having to pack it away the next morning.

Dot's been parked in the garage next door. She's not moved much since we've been back, now six months ago. She can't — I think she's completely seized up — so for the time being she's wrapped beneath a blanket until I have the money and the knowledge to repair her. I would like to fix her; she deserves to be fixed. In the meantime I've been riding around on the C90 I was going to do the trip on in the first place. It's not as cool as Dot and no way do I think that would have made it across the world, but it's been good to take a break from the book every now and again, riding through the Yorkshire Dales and up the coast, passing through the towns of Scarborough and Whitby. At other times I have even equipped her with the panniers from Dot and ridden further afield, often visiting friends.

It's been great to catch up with everyone. As anyone who's ever been away for any length of time will testify, it's surprising how quickly you can slip back into a social group as though you've never been away. Talk turns quickly to what they've been up to and who's been dating who and what the new hairdresser looks like and so on, until you forget you've even been away. But it has been much harder this time. I suppose this journey has been my life, I have nothing else in it, I have nothing else much to contribute and that leaves me staring off into the distance thinking of the Outback or the Kazakh steppe, sometimes to the point that I wish I'd never seen them at all, as I might be more content with the current view if I hadn't.

I really miss those conversations I had in Pakistan, sitting around that table, or around the camp fire in Malaysia, or anywhere else there's been a nice group. I also miss that feeling of being on the brink, that taste of danger and that moment when you feel most alive. It's like taking a drug you can never have again, unless of course you're prepared to venture even further into danger in order to find some more. That might be why I don't end up listening to my mum, who still tells me to grow up and settle down. Though I know, now more than ever, that I need to. Writing this book has made me confront that truth. It's perhaps why at times I wish I'd not had it to write, or even had the story to tell. Ignorance is bliss, as they say. I shall certainly not miss the keyboard. I shall not miss living in the past. And talk of change is stupid. I think we only adapt.

In other news the Frenchman kidnapped in Pakistan has been released and so far, of everyone I met on my travels, all made it back in one piece. The two German cyclists in East Timor, Sven and Caroline, arrived home a good year after I'd met them, and the last I heard of Nat and Aki on the other postie bike, they were in Japan. Michel, Andrew and Amelia, from Pakistan, finished their journeys, and even Daniel, entering Afghanistan in his 4x4, got through okay, posting some incredible pictures from that country. He said it was completely safe in the north and fascinating to see a different reality from that portrayed in the media. I gather he's in Georgia with no plans to come home yet. The Hülsmanns, Andreas and Claudia, they're doing fine. Nazgul, the girl in the Bishkek shop, made it to London and is studying English. Joe and the gang at One Ten Motorcycles have moved into new premises, and sadly Kevin Rudd is no longer Prime Minister of Australia having been forced out by Julia Gillard.

What's saddened me most since I got back is hearing of the terrible events happening in the places I passed through. First there was Bangkok with more of those riots, this time with so many more killed. Also Kyrgyzstan, where the death toll from a sudden wave of ethnic tension reached triple figures, and reduced the beautiful town of Osh to cinders. It seemed such a peaceful country, I can't understand it. Nazgul couldn't either; her family was affected. There's also been more trouble in Pakistan, more bombs and more blasts, and then the dreadful flooding that has swamped one-fifth of the land and left millions homeless. When I see the images on the news I feel for them. The people in those countries were good to me, the best. Then to be at a local petrol station the other night and hear a moron shout, 'Rag head' from his car to a girl behind me wearing a veil had me wonder how a foreigner would fare travelling through 'our' world on a motorbike. They certainly wouldn't be high-fived from the roadside, that's for sure.

As for me and Mandy, we're still in touch, still friends, on opposite sides of the world again. Of course I miss her dearly and often resent myself for being the type of person who might want to do a trip like this, because then I think maybe things would have worked out better between us. Though if I'd have been a more settled person then I wouldn't have been in Australia at speed-dating in the first place. You can't help your nature, as my nan might say. And she's right, as she always is, and also a little better now. But I guess sometimes you have to — help your nature that is — otherwise you might spend your whole life searching for something that doesn't exist. And end up with nothing. So it's a balancing act. But who knows what's around the next corner or over the next horizon? Maybe the next challenge, or a new road. Or just maybe, a full stop.

Acknowledgements

It would be difficult to thank everyone by name as so many people were responsible for my safe passage across the world. But to everyone who helped, supported, or even just allowed me to ride past without causing a fuss, thank you. More specifically I'd like to thank my brother Jason for setting up a website at short notice (www.thepostman.org.uk), and also Paul Taylor, a legend, and a great friend, for all the advice, wisdom and support you've offered me over the years. I couldn't have done it without you. Thank you also the online community: ADVRider in particular, the support and encouragement you offered to a total stranger was overwhelming. Also mention for Horizons Unlimited and London Biker for the extra support and advice. Glad I was able to take you along for the ride.

Soichiro Honda, thank you for building a bike that gave me the confidence to do the trip. Thank you also to the people who sponsored me as I went along; together we collected over $1000 for Comic Relief. Special mention also for Joe and the gang at One Ten Motorcycles in Caboolture, my friends in Mansfield — Mark, Neil, Jim, Aaron, William, Katy, Gemma, Olesja, Louise, Chris — and also those in Australia — Rowan and Shannon (for the gloves), Matty and Sal for the gloves and map, Tommy for stealing the milk crate, Katie, Kylie, and especially Lucy, who's idea it was to go speed-dating in the first place. Karen, of ABC Books, thank you for taking interest in the guy on the postie bike riding across the world. Thank you also for not letting me quit when I asked to. Also John, my editor, for your honesty. It was needed. And last but not least, the Real Mandy, for making me want to be better, and do better. I love you always. Now go and be happy.